SELF-CARE:
THE NEED AND
A MODEL

A Theological and Scriptural Framework

Dr. B.G. Edison

WESTBOW
PRESS®
A DIVISION OF THOMAS NELSON
& ZONDERVAN

WestBow Press books may be ordered through booksellers or by contacting:

WestBow Press
A Division of Thomas Nelson & Zondervan
1663 Liberty Drive
Bloomington, IN 47403
www.westbowpress.com
844-714-3454

Scripture quotations are taken from the Holy Bible, New International Version®, NIV®. Copyright © 1973, 1978, 1984 by Biblica, Inc.™ Used by permission of Zondervan. All rights reserved worldwide.

ISBN: 979-8-3850-0579-6 (sc)
ISBN: 979-8-3850-0580-2 (e)

Library of Congress Control Number: 2023916285

Print information available on the last page.

WestBow Press rev. date: 9/11/2023

To Cecelia (Proverbs 31:10-11), my answer to prayer for a wife.
No one else could understand and know me like you do; No
one else could be my love-no one else but you!

To my gifts from God, my children, Chloe and Benjamin.
Thank you all for being so understanding and supportive while I conducted research.

Praise be to the God and Father of our Lord Jesus Christ, the Father of compassion
and the God of all comfort, who comforts us in all our troubles, so that we can
comfort those in any trouble with the comfort we ourselves have received from God.
2 Corinthians 1:3-4

CONTENTS

ABSTRACT

SELF-CARE: THE NEED AND A MODEL

A THEOLOGICAL AND SCRIPTURE FRAMEWORK

Issue: This paper addresses the directive from the United States Army Chief of Chaplain as stated in the United States Army Chaplain Corps Strategic Campaign Plan, 2008-2013. The goal is to strengthen the spiritual life of the Army Chaplaincy during a period of persistent conflict. One way to accomplish this is to include a spiritual development plan in every Chaplain Officer Evaluation Report (OER) Support Form 67-9-1b. This study is designed to flush out the spiritual development plan from the aspect of self-care; to identify the need for self-care and to present a model. Self-care can be defined as the acknowledgement of one's spiritual, mental, and physical (soul, mind, and body) preparedness to conduct life changing ministry. It is the care needed to maintain effective job performance and holistic wellness. The chaplain is a clergy person ordained by God to provide and perform ministry in a military milieu. The demands of the military are great and unique. To provide and perform ministry globally in this demanding military surrounding is challenging. To maintain spiritual wholeness and resist becoming fragmented involves innovation in self-care.

Thesis: To identify the need for self-care in the United States Army Chaplain Corps and to present a model of self-care. To strengthen the spiritual life of the Chaplain Corps self-care is a necessity. A healthy chaplain will benefit the Department of Defense, military organizations, family members and themselves. Self-care is needed not only because of the demands of the military and its uniqueness, but also is due to the fact that the chaplain is called to holiness. The implied task to conduct self-care for military chaplains is given in the United States Army Chaplain Corps Strategic Campaign Plan, 2008-2013 and the Covenant and Code of Ethics for Chaplains of the Armed Forces. The Covenant and Code of Ethics for Chaplains of the Armed Forces is provided by the armed forces ecclesiastical endorsing agents.

Application: The pastoral research project was designed to be used in support of the United States Army Chaplain Corps Strategic Campaign Plan, 2008-2013. The research design consisted of questionnaires and interviews from United States Army, Navy, and Air Force Chaplains, and civilian clergy. Data was collected through permission granted interviews and questionnaires. This qualitative research helped to confirm the hypothesis (there is a need of a formal and/or informal model of self-care in the United States Army Chaplaincy) and develop a Christian/religious component to be used as an option in the United States Army Chaplain Corps Strategic Campaign Plan, 2008-2013, which is nested with the four strategic goals of the Army Campaign Plan. This new component and this accepted model will better equip the chaplain to conduct self-care thus, assisting the chaplaincy of accomplishing its goal of strengthening the spiritual life of the United States Army Chaplaincy.

INTRODUCTION

The United States Army is a professional organization. United States Army chaplains are a part of this professional organization. The United States Army Chaplain Corps was born 29 July 1775. Chaplains have a unique moral role in the Army. Throughout these two hundred and thirty three years, the United States Army Chaplain has helped American Soldiers deal with the rigors of combat and the demands of military life. Approximately twenty five thousand Army Chaplains have served as religious and spiritual leaders for twenty million Soldiers and their families. Their mission is clear: to bring God to the Soldier and the Soldier to God. The chaplain makes personal sacrifices for God and country daily.

The chaplain is exposed to the same physical, mental, and spiritual challenges the Soldiers endure. One unique characteristic that sets chaplains apart from civilian clergy is the responsibility to deploy in a combat theater. Chaplains form a unique bond and relationship because they are side by side on the front lines with their parishioners. When units deploy, people deploy, and when people deploy, chaplains deploy to provide pastoral care. This gives the chaplain the unique opportunity to know and be known by the Soldiers they serve. This enables critical access to them during times of crisis. On a daily basis, chaplains are placed in harm's way. The question is not will chaplains be affected by the ugliness of war, but when and how much? There is no other military helping agency in the military that can complete the work of a chaplain. This is why it is important to offer a self-care model to better prepare United States Army Chaplains to provide and perform ministry.

In order to be the spiritual backbone of out fighting force, the chaplains must care for themselves spiritual. The chaplain is called to holiness by God. What happens when the chaplain becomes fragmented and his or her ministry becomes stifled?

Are the self-care techniques the chaplain uses adequate or inadequate? What are some of the presuppositions? One example of this is the idea of selfless service, which is one of the Army's Seven Values. The understanding behind selfless service is to place the mission and others before our own. The question stands, when is the 'self' or the individual able to find balance? Where do they stand in the equation? Selfless service many times equates to "useless service." Often times it is extremely difficult for the chaplain to practice what they preach, to talk the talk and to walk the walk.

The design of the research is to explore the issues both internal and external that prevent self-care and offer some preventative measure techniques. The research will show the causes and symptoms of compassion fatigue and burnout, which are enemies of self-care.

The author believes the role of a chaplain is a calling from God. When God calls the minister to a military vocation as a chaplain God will continue to equip the chaplain for duty. Due to our humanity and frailty the chaplain is not perfect. The chaplain is in constant pursuit of improving and strengthening themselves in the area of self-care. Self-care is an individual responsibility.

There is a theological view of self-care. This paper will explore some specific Christian views of self-care and present a paradigm providing this specific pastoral model that is rooted in Christian theology. The theological research for this paper will consist of a study from the Old and New Testaments, looking at the foundation and interpretation of self-care. It will examine biblical examples of Jesus Christ modeling self-care; one who always brought balance to His ministry. For the Christian Chaplain, remembering that God is in control comes in nurturing trust in Jesus Christ in the midst of stress and persecution.

The pastoral research project for this paper will present a model of self-care. This model is simple enough to be used daily. The intent of the author was to establish a model that has feasibility. The model can be memorized and used in any ministry environment. Conducting self-care in any environment is challenging. The difficulty increases when conducted in a military milieu. Conducting self-care is not impossible, but takes some innovation. Jesus Christ offered the self-care model of rest, quiet place, benefits of fellowship, and remembering that God is in control. Saint Mark gives the account of Jesus calming a storm (Mark 4: 35-41). The scriptures illustrate Jesus successfully conducting self-care on the boat during the storm. Life often times brings many storms. Conducting self-care will help the chaplain rest in the storm.

CHAPTER ONE

PASTORAL CHALLENGE

This paper addresses the challenge of military clergy, particularly U.S. Army Chaplains, to conduct self-care in a demanding military environment. Self-care can be defined as the acknowledgment of who one is spiritually, mentally, and physically (soul, mind, and body), and the care needed to maintain effectiveness in all areas. The demands of the military are great. Today, our nation is at war. This country is in a long struggle against terrorism both foreign and domestic; a struggle that has reached our homeland and has become known as the Global War On Terrorism (GWOT). The demands from GWOT are numerous. The military is carrying the burden of fighting wars on two fronts: in Iraq and Afghanistan. It is charged also is with reinforcing political relationships in Liberia, Haiti, and Djibouti, Africa. The military is also preparing for contingencies in North Korea and Iran, and supporting peacekeeping operations in Bosnia, Kosovo, and Sinai.

Providing and performing ministry in this demanding military is exciting, challenging and rewarding. To maintain spiritual wholeness, balance and to resist becoming fragmented and broken involves innovation in caring for ones self. It takes more for chaplains to be spiritually whole because of the enormous stressors in the military. What more must chaplains' do in the area of self-care to avoid becoming fragmented? It takes daily care for the caregiver to transition from being the "walking wounded" to the wounded healer.

Self-care is a must in any form of ministry, particularly the military. The Covenant and the Code of Ethics for Chaplains of the Armed Forces and Chaplain Corps Strategic Campaign Plan, 2008-2013 mandates, is it a guide or is it implied that chaplains conduct self-care. The armed forces ecclesiastical endorsing agents provide the Covenant and Code of Ethics for Chaplains of the Armed Forces. The Covenant and Code of Ethics for Chaplains of the Armed Forces is listed below and the specific self-care passage will be italicized:

The Covenant

Having accepted God's Call to minister to people who serve in the armed forces of our country, I covenant to serve God and these people with God's help; to deepen my obedience to the commandments, to love the Lord our God with all my heart, soul, mind and strength, and to love my neighbor as myself. In affirmation of this commitment, I will abide by the Code of Ethics for chaplains of the United States Armed Forces, and I will faithfully support its purpose and ideals. As further affirmation of my commitment, I covenant with my colleagues in ministry that we will hold one another accountable for fulfillment of all public actions set forth in our Code of Ethics.

The Code of Ethics

I will hold in trust the traditions and practices of my religious body.

I will carefully adhere to whatever direction may be conveyed to me by my endorsing body for maintenance of my endorsement.

I will understand as a chaplain in the United States Armed Forces that I will function in a pluralistic environment with chaplains of other religious bodies to provide for ministry to all military personnel and their families entrusted to my care.

I will seek to provide for pastoral care and ministry to persons of religious bodies other than my own within my area of responsibility with the same investment of myself as I give to members of my own religious body. I will work collegially with chaplains of religious bodies other than my own as together we seek to provide as full a ministry as possible to our people. I will respect the beliefs and traditions of my colleagues and those to whom I minister. When conducting services of worship that include persons of other than my religious body, I will draw upon those beliefs, principles, and practices that we have in common.

I will, if in a supervisory position, respect the practices and beliefs of each chaplain I supervise and exercise care not to require of them any service or practice that would be in violation of the faith practices of their particular religious body.

I will seek to support all colleagues in ministry by building constructive relationships wherever I serve, both with the staff where I work and with colleagues throughout the military environment.

I will maintain a disciplined ministry in such ways as keeping hours of prayer and devotion, endeavoring to maintain wholesome family relationships and regularly engaging in educational and recreational activities for professional and personal development. I will seek to maintain good health habits.

I will recognize that my obligation is to provide for the free exercise of religion for ministry to all members of the military services, their families and other authorized personnel. When on active duty, I will only accept added responsibility in civilian ministry if it does not interfere with the overall effectiveness of my primary military ministry.

I will defend my colleagues against unfair discrimination on the basis of gender, race, religion or national origin.

I will hold in confidence my privileged communication received by me during the conduct of my ministry. I will not disclose confidential communication in private or in public.

I will not proselytize from other religious bodies, but I retain the right to evangelize those who are not affiliated.

I will show personal love for God in my life and ministry, as I strive together with my colleagues to preserve the dignity, maintain the discipline and promote the integrity of the profession to which we have been called.

I recognize the special power afforded me by my ministerial office. I will never use that power in ways that violate the personhood of another human being, religiously, emotionally or sexually. I will use my pastoral office only for that which is best for the persons under my ministry.[1]

The servant of God needs to be whole for the benefit of self, family, and providing pastoral care to others. Other leaders and Soldiers in the chaplain's chain of command can follow the chaplain's examples of self-care to reach wholeness and to maintain wholeness.

The U.S. Army 20th Chief of Chaplains instituted a strategic plan to develop a deeper spiritual life in the Unit Ministry Team. Under "Spiritual Leadership Goals and Objectives" 1.1.1, 1.1.2, and 1.1.7, the mandate states:

---

[1] A project of the National Conference on Ministry to the Armed Forces (NCMAF), February 2003.

Initiate a program to train total chaplaincy on how to give and receive spiritual direction by 4th quarter FY 2001. Initiate a program to include a spiritual development plan in every chaplain's Officer Evaluation Report (OER) Support Form 67-9-1 by 4th quarter FY 2001...Conduct spiritual development workshops and retreats at each installation for Unit Ministry Teams and family members by 4th quarter FY 2001.[2]

The 22th Chief of Chaplains of the U.S. Army enhanced the Chaplain Corps Strategic Campaign Plan, 2008-2013 to fulfill its collective calling to meet the religious and spiritual needs of America's Army. Army Goal number two states: Train and equip Soldiers and grow adaptive leaders. Chaplaincy objective, 2.1, supports the Army Goal number two. The Chaplaincy objective, 2.1 reads: Develop Army Chaplains and Chaplain Assistants that are Spiritually Fit and Focused to Support the Mission. A supporting mandate reads:

Include a spiritual development plan in every Chaplain Officer Evaluation Report (OER) Support Form 67-9-1b. Conduct annual spiritual development workshops or retreats at institutional level and above for UMT and family members.[3]

What is hindering self-care? Is caring for ones self being hindered? Some chaplains have never heard of the term self-care, others have never heard of the Covenant and the Code of Ethics for Chaplains of the Armed Forces and / or the Chaplain Corps Strategic Campaign Plan, 2008-2013, while others struggle with trying to establish a model. I believe chaplains see the need for spiritual well-being, but struggle with the how to conduct self renewal or what a specific model of self-care looks like.

Target Audience

Chaplains are pastors serving in the military community. The Chaplain is a qualified and endorsed clergy person of a DOD (Department of Defense) recognized religious denomination or faith group.[4] "Chaplains are required by law to hold religious services for members of the command to which they are assigned, when practicable. (Title 10, United States Code, section 3547)[5] This includes garrison, contingency operations, and battlefield

---

[2] U.S. Army Chief of Chaplains, The U.S. Army Chaplaincy Strategic Plan FY 2000-2005, (Washington, D.C.: Government Printing Office, August, 2000), 11.

[3] U.S. Army Chief of Chaplains, The U.S. Army Chaplaincy Strategic Plan FY 2008-2013, (Washington, D.C.: Government Printing Office, March, 2007).

[4] Army Regulation 165-1, Religious Activities: Chaplain Activities in the United States Army. (Washington, D.C. Government Printing Office, 1998) 4-3 (b).

[5] Ibid, Chp 4, 4-4 (a).

conditions. Chaplains provide for religious support, pastoral care, and the moral and ethical well-being of the command.[6]

Self-Care Defined

Defining individual self-care will take an individual on a journey, a journey in search of our significance. To truly define self-care, the individual must define self. The individual must understand himself or herself. They must know their likes and dislikes and their strengths and areas of improvements or weaknesses. Once the individual understands himself or herself they can better define what self-care is for them personally. As mentioned earlier self-care is a journey and it starts with a search for significance. "An accurate understanding of God's truth is the first step toward discovering our significance and worth."[7]

Simply stated, self-care is the acknowledgment of who one is spiritually, mentally, and physically (soul, mind, and body), and the care needed to maintain effectiveness in all areas. Self-care is a preventative measure, towards holistic wellness. Spiritual fitness is an individual responsibility, as well as, the responsibility of the organization. "You, the individual, can do more for your own health and well being than any doctor, any hospital, any drug, and any exotic medical devices."[8] Spiritual accountability involves practicing prevention and taking personal responsibility for one's own health.

Applicable Self-Care Strategies

Numerous resources are available in the area of self-care for civilian pastors. Two models give particular help in this area. One book of great value is entitled, "Rest in the Storm: Self-Care Strategies for Clergy and Other Caregivers" by Dr. Kirk Jones.[9] Dr. Jones offered three basic strategies for slowing down. First, he advised leisure time, suggesting to, "Go to the back of the boat" (a reference to Matthew 8:24-27). Second, he advised, move at your own pace: a slow, deliberate, mindful, and "sacred pace" (also a reference to Matthew 8: 24-27 and to John 11:6). Dr. Jones referred to Jesus' refusal to rush, even when the world around him imposed a sense of urgency: sometimes, Jesus waited. "In the waiting," Dr. Jones said, "the truth comes; as agonizing as waiting can be, deeper truth comes." He also urged his readers to take time to notice more, listen more, and think more deeply. "Practice

---

[6] Ibid, Chp. 4, 4-4 (a).

[7] Robert S. McGee, The Search for Significance, (Houston, Texas: Rapha, 1990), 14.

[8] Donald D. Vickery and James F. Fries, Take Care of Yourself, (Massachusetts: Addison-Wesley Publishing Company, Inc., 1989), xxi.

[9] Kirk Byron Jones, Rest In The Storm: Self-Care Strategies for Clergy and Other Caregivers, Valley Forge, PA: Judson Press, 2001).

the pause," he said. Third, he stated, be still: Learn to cultivate stillness. Jesus (Matthew 8: 24-27) challenged the storm to stop itself. "We are," Dr. Jones suggested, "walking storms," and he added, we must claim the power to be still.

Another book entitled, "You Don't Have To Go Home From Work Exhausted" by Ann McGee-Cooper gives another model. Mrs. McGee-Cooper writes about burnout symptoms and mentions, "A vital key is to realize that burnout is not something that happens only once in a lifetime."[10] She mentions that burnout is the result of living out of balance. She identifies three profiles that lead to burnout-perfectionism, "fast-lane" living, and the superhuman syndrome. Mrs. McGee-Cooper describes a perfectionist as one who performs all tasks equally meticulously well. She goes on to illustrate "fast-lane" living by using the Indianapolis (Indy) 500 analogy. The Indy 500 is a major race car competition in the United States where competitive race cars travel 500 miles full throttle at top speeds. Many times people run their lives at top speeds with minimal pit stops versus a full overhaul. Lastly, Mrs. McGee-Cooper describes the superhuman syndrome. "The most basic underlying compulsion for superhumans is to be all things to all people."[11]

Mrs. McGee-Cooper lists twelve cures for burnout: proper rest, eating for high performance and peak energy, daily fun "nonstressed" aerobic exercise, time alone, time to read and learn, spiritual growth, intimacy and love, fun-joy-play, quality time with family and friends, new hobbies and old hobbies, regular and frequent vacations, and sense of purpose.[12]

The U.S. Army Chaplain Corps and the endorsing agents have identified the need for spiritual betterment. The chaplain must determine for themselves what self-care looks like. Even with the self-care guideline from the ecclesiastical endorsing agents and the Chief of Chaplains each chaplain will still struggle and face opposition when trying to conduct self-care. The main reason for this struggle is due to the nature of the environment the chaplain ministers in. The military offers unique struggles and present unique enemies to self-care. Conducting self-care is not impossible, but it will take being innovative to meet the need for the chaplain as he or she ministers in the unique military environment. Being vigilant with self-care is not impossible, but developing it will take intentionality. The chaplain must improvise, adapt and overcome their opposing circumstances to maintain wholeness in order to minister to their flock.

---

[10] Alice McGee-Cooper, You Do Not Have To Go Home Exhausted, (New York, N.Y.: Bantam Books, 1992), 122.
[11] Ibid, 150.
[12] Ibid, 175.

CHAPTER TWO

WHY THE NEED FOR SELF-CARE

Introduction

In chapter one, self-care was defined as the acknowledgement of who one is spiritually, mentally, and physically (soul, mind, and body) and the care needed to maintain effective job performance and holistic wellness in all areas. Being spiritually fragmented can present itself in the form of compassion fatigue and particularly burnout.

The core doctrinal principles of the Chaplain Corp are: nurturing the living, caring for the wounded, and honoring the dead.[13] In these three core doctrinal principles, there is an implied task of nurturing the living-the chaplains themselves.

Self-care is a natural basic part of life survival. It is an ethical failing not to conduct self-care as a minister because the call to holiness by God. When chaplains do not conduct self-care they practice self-neglect and flirt with disaster. September 11, 2001, (9-11)[14] was an eye opener to the evil that lurks in this world. After 9-11, societies started preparing themselves for unknown acts of evil. People flocked to purchase gas mask in preparation for a possible nuclear, chemical or biological attack. The military community, particular the U.S. Army, has always had to maintain a ready state of vigilance. The "the military is here to fight and win America's wars" is one of our mottos. The military is meant to be a deterrent to evil. Chaplains live in and minister in this type of milieu. Self-care is extremely important to keep chaplains from becoming depleted in the areas of cognition, emotional, behavioral, spiritual, physical, interpersonal relationships, and work performance. A chaplain's failure to nurture themselves leads to a reduced relationship with God, self, family and the people to whom they minister.

---

[13] Reference Book 16-100, The Unit Ministry Team Handbook, (Washington, D.C.: Government Printing Office, 1998), 1-2.

[14] For the remainder of this book I will refer to September 11, 2001 as 9-11.

Challenges to Self-Care

Caring is costly, especially caring for those in a war theater and those returning to home base. There will be individuals suffering from physical wounds and non-visible scars such as Post Traumatic Stress Disorder (PTSD). USA Today released an article that stated, "a fifth of Soldiers are at risk of PTSD."[15] The report by the Army Medical Command showed as the number of deployments for Soldiers to Iraq and Afghanistan increase so does the Soldiers chances of emotional illnesses. Chaplains are at the forefront providing ministry to these Soldiers who show signs of depression and/or PTSD. These psychological wounds also affect the Soldiers families. The findings of the Army mental health study go on to say about two in ten Soldiers say their marriages are in trouble.

Empathetic professionals who listen to the stories of fear, pain and suffering of others may feel similar fear, pain and suffering. Professionals especially vulnerable to compassion fatigue include emergency care workers, counselors, mental heath professionals, medical professionals, volunteers, mortuary affairs workers, clergy, and chaplains. If one of these caregivers ever feels that they are becoming interwoven emotionally with their clients they possibly could be suffering from compassion fatigue.

The concept of compassion fatigue emerged only in the last several years in the professional literature. It identifies the cost of caring for traumatized people. Compassion fatigue is the emotional residue of exposure to working with the suffering, particularly those suffering from the consequences of traumatic events. A professional who works with people, particularly people who are suffering, must contend not only with the normal stress or dissatisfaction of work, but also the emotional and personal feelings for the suffering.[16]

Compassion fatigue can be defined, as a state of tension and preoccupation with the individual or cumulative trauma of clients.[17] Compassion fatigue manifest itself in one or more ways: re-experiencing the traumatic events, avoidance/numbing of reminders of the traumatic event, and persistent arousal.[18] Persistent arousal is the absorption and retention the emotional suffering of others in interaction with other experiences, past and present.

Although compassion fatigue is similar to critical incident stress (being traumatized by something actually experienced or seen), with compassion fatigue a caregiver absorbs the trauma through the eyes and ears of the client. It is a secondary post-traumatic stress. The human costs of compassion fatigue are lowered job performance, more mistakes and flagging morale. Personal relationships are also affected and eventually an overall decline in the general health of the care giver may occur.

---

[15] USA Today, "A fifth of Soldiers at PTSD risk." 7 March 2008, 11A.

[16] Didactic taught by Chaplain (LTC) Al Gales, "Trauma Ministry." Walter Reed Army Medical Center, 5 December 2003.

[17] Didactic taught by Ms. Victoria Burner, "Compassion Fatigue." Deployment Health Clinical Center, Walter Reed Army Medical Center, 31 March 2004.

[18] Didactic taught by Ms. Victoria Burner, "Compassion Fatigue." Deployment Health Clinical Center, Walter Reed Army Medical Center, 14 April 2004.

Physical symptoms of compassion fatigue and burnout of being accident prone, change in eating habits and weight, chronic fatigue, exhaustion, headaches, high blood pressure, increased susceptibility to illness, and intolerance to sensory stimuli. Emotional symptoms consist of anxiety, discouragement, disillusionment with the organization, emotional exhaustion, feelings of failure, self-blame and self-pity, feelings of having nothing left to give, inability to enjoy leisure activities, irritability, loss of coping skills, loss of emotional control, loss of humor, loss of self-esteem and self-confidence, and social withdrawal (disconnection). Mental symptoms consist of anxiety, decreased efficiency, detachment, forgetfulness, inability to reach decisions, inability to concentrate, loss of motivation, mental exhaustion, perception of failure, and rejection. Spiritual symptoms consist of being angry with God, disillusioned with the church, doubting your call to the ministry, increased expectations and demands, isolation, lack of accountability, Messiah and Martyr Complex, stagnation and staleness, struggling with commitment to both God and ministry, unable to pray, unable to study the Bible and have devotions, and questioning your faith[19].

Burnout is the syndrome which is the cumulative effects of stress involved with ones care giving. A frequent vacation or change of job helps a great deal. Christina Maslach provided the primary study of burnout during the early 1970s. Her research concluded that the three significant elements of burnout are emotional exhaustion, depersonalization and reduced personal accomplishment.[20]

Ms. Maslach burnout syndromes of emotional exhaustion, depersonalization and reduced personal accomplishment have a downward spiral effect. The first aspect of the burnout syndrome is emotional exhaustion. Emotional exhaustion is the feeling of being overwhelmed emotionally by the demands imposed by people. A major downside to emotional exhaustion is becoming callous emotionally, a disregard to the needs and feelings of others. Her second aspect of the burnout syndrome is depersonalization. Depersonalization is when a provider becomes so emotionally exhausted that they start developing a poor opinion of the people they are assisting. At times they fail to provide adequate care and start mistreating others. These feelings can turn inwardly and the caregiver may begin feeling guilty about the way they treated the person seeking service. The finally aspect of her burnout syndrome is reduced personal accomplishment. Feelings of reduced personal accomplishments carry over from becoming an uncaring person during the second aspect of the burnout syndrome-depersonalization. Self-imposed feelings of failure, inadequacy and low self-esteem start surfacing.[21] Negative self-criticism limits the creativity of the provider.

---

[19] Didactic taught by Chaplain (LTC) Al Gales, "Trauma Ministry." Walter Reed Army Medical Center, 5 December 2003.

[20] Christina Maslach, Burnout: The Cost of Caring. (Cambridge, MA: Malor Books, 2003), 10.

[21] Ibid, 2-8.

"Clergy burnout results from overwork and blurred pastoral identity."[22] To some degree, everyone experiences some sort of burnout each day. Problems come when burnout is serious and sustained and the ability to function as a chaplain is impaired. Maslach suggests that burnout is gradual and is an erosion of the human soul.[23] Her analysis can be compared to a slow leaking tire verses a blowout. A slow leak is progressive, it takes time. A blowout happens suddenly. Burnout is the slow leak that needs repaired before an emergency happens.

The burnout is a relative new term. The metaphor of burnout originated in the physical sciences not in the social sciences. The shift to use the term in the social sciences occurred about four decades ago. Joseph Sittler, a Lutheran theologian, wrote an essay in 1961 titled "Maceration of the Minister." He choose the term *macerate*, which means to chop up into small pieces, to give the thesis of his essay shock value. Sittler proposes that "the minister's time, focused sense of vocation, vision of his or her central task, mental life and contemplative acreage are all under the chopper. The minister had reached this poor state of affairs because of pressures emanating from the parish, the general church bodies (denominations), and the self-image of the minister."[24]

John A. Sanford points out that Webster's New International Dictionary defined burnout in the terms of something that happens in the natural world and not to humans. Rather, burnout referred to one of these possibilities: "First, the word can refer to the burning out of the interior or contents of something, such as a building. Second, it can be used in the field of electricity to refer to the breakdown of a circuit owing to combustion caused by high temperatures; in this case, the conductor has been burned out by the high temperatures produced by the electric current. Third, it can be used in forestry to refer to a forest floor that has been destroyed leaving the forest denuded."[25] As mentioned before these definitions all relate to the physical sciences and not social sciences.

Also the Diagnostic and Statistical Manual of Mental Disorders, Fourth Edition (DSM-IV), indicates that burnout is not a psychological disorder. It falls under Axis IV: Psychosocial and Environmental Problems, and is caused by environmental issues. Problems such as unemployment, threat of job loss, stressful work schedule, difficult working conditions, job dissatisfaction, job change, and discord with boss or co-workers are grouped under the category of occupational problems.[26] Burnout is a temporary disability that prevents one from effective job performance.

---

[22] Joe E. Trull and James C. Carter, Ministerial Ethics: Being a Good Minister in a Not-So-Good World, (Nashville: Broadman, 1983), 21.

[23] Maslach, 17.

[24] Joseph Sittler, The Maceration of the Minister. In Grace Notes and Other Fragments, selected and edited by Robert M. Herhold and Linda Marie Dellhoff, Philadelphia: Fortess, 57-68, 1981.

[25] John A. Sanford, Ministry Burnout. (New York: Paulist Press, 1982), 2-3.

[26] Diagnostic Statistical Manual, Fourth Edition, 41-43.

G. Lloyd Rediger, a long-time pastoral counselor offers a clinical perspective on burnout. He believes burnout presents itself in the form of many characteristics of depression, thus requiring specialized attention and treatment. Rediger suggest that a combination of two or more from each category of specific symptoms usually identifies the individual suffering from the burnout syndrome. The symptoms are:

> Physically. Exhausted appearance. Frequent headaches and gastric upset. Hypochondcriacal complaints. Loss of sexual vigor. Low energy. Motor difficulties such as a lack of coordination, tremors, twitches. Significant change in sleep patterns. Weight change.

> Emotionally. Apathy. Constant irritability. Constant worry. Complaints of loneliness. Excessive crying. Hopelessness. Inability to be playful or become interested in diversionary activities. Loss of humor or development of 'gallows humor.' One-track mind and loss of creativity. Paranoid obsessions. Random thought patterns and inability to concentrate. Sporadic efforts to act as if everything is back to normal.

> Spiritually. Cynicism. Development of moral judgmentalism. Drastic changes in theological statements. Listless and perfunctory performance of clergy-role duties. Loss of faith in God, the church, and themselves. Loss of joy and celebration in spiritual endeavors. Loss of prayer and meditational disciplines. One-track preaching and teaching. Significant changes in moral behavior.[27]

Causes of Burnout and Compassion Fatigue

There are several challenges unique to the chaplain when trying to initiate self-care. First, inter-personal and social factors will be discussed. Inter-personal factors involve relations between people. Inter-personal factors under discussion are chaplains as crisis people, expectations of others, society's example of self-care, and efforts of building awareness. Second, the intra-personal and individual factors contributing to burnout and/or compassion fatigue will be explored. Intra-personal factors occur within the individual's self. Intra-personal factors under discussion are maintaining health through, diet, exercise, and rest, functioning on one's persona, overfunctioning, and the reality of human sinfulness. Finally, we shall discuss ways in which not only factors in one's military surroundings lead to burnout and/or compassion fatigue, but also, how does a person contribute to experiencing burnout and/or compassion fatigue.

---

[27] G. Lloyd Rediger, Coping with Clergy Burnout. (Judson Press: Valley Forge, PA., 1982), 16-17.

Inter-Personal Factors

Chaplains are 'crisis' orientated. Chaplains are involved in pain, life and death situations daily, perhaps more than any other profession. In clinical settings chaplains increase their involvement with the dying and continue to minister to the bereaved. Any sustained amount of crisis ministry without proper self-care can undermine ministry attempts.

The 'expectations of others' are one of the most frequently cited factor that leads to burnout and compassion fatigue in ministers.[28] "Perhaps in no other profession, except maybe that of the politician," writes John Sanford, "is a person facing so many expectations from so many people, and, to make the situations more complicated, the expectations people place upon the ministering person vary enormously."[29]

The stress factors for clergy include the sheer number of expectations, the variety of expectations and the changing nature of these expectations. Mr. Sanford describes the array of expectations the minister must juggle, which may apply to men or women:

> Some people expect the priest or minister to be a great teacher, others want
> him foremost to be a faithful pastor, others hand him the task of being a
> financial wizard, some want him to maintain the old traditions, but just as
> many may want him to be pleasingly avant garde (yet not threaten them too
> much!). Some expect him to devote himself to calling on the sick, or making
> parish calls, or attending community social functions, or being concerned
> with the poor or civil rights, while others want him for a personal counselor,
> or want him to be a famous preacher. Because these expectations come from
> the people who are simultaneously the minister's flock (parishioners) and
> employers-"they are the ones who pay the bills"-the minister has no choice
> but to reckon with these expectations.[30]

Our 'society does not do a good job of setting the example of performing self-care.'[31] Ours is a self-centered society. Thus chaplains are influenced by the society as a whole. Members of other professions suffer from self-neglect and burnout trying to reach the top in an expedient manner. The promotion of self-care, in general, in society is abundant, but numerous opposing forces dwarf the attempts. "People who run, run, run and work, work, and work are not the most productive and creative persons in our society."[32] Long work hours, working overtime, losing annual leave, missing vacations, not being able to attend special family events are examples of self-neglect and are all part of the expected workers

---

[28] Sanford, 32.
[29] Ibid, 7.
[30] Ibid, 7-8.
[31] Eliot A. Cohen, <u>Our Soldiers and Us,</u> Washington Post Article, May 25, 2004, A17.
[32] Jones, 108.

life. Employees in corporate America experience these problems due to the competitive nature of their surroundings. Many times workers will neglect their self nurturance for the highs of success. The world says, 'Climb the ladder of success, even if it means sacrificing one's well-being.'

Medical specialists in the medical field combat occupational stress routinely and the individual need for health stress reduction. Trauma personnel consist of, trauma nurses, emergency workers and crisis counselors; have struggled to recognize their vulnerability to compassion fatigue and burnout and solutions to their symptoms. If the general public has this struggle, it is natural that the military will adopt the same or similar well being struggles.

The military turns civilians into civilian Soldiers, thus these people entering the military will enter with a misunderstood definition of self-care. Society and the military, at times do an inadequate job of self-care and this view spirals down to the chaplaincy. The chaplaincy informally advocates self-care, but according to the United States Army Chaplain Center and School (USACHCS) there is no significant training module for the chaplain attending the basic and advance courses. USACHCS is the central training center for all Chaplain Corps personnel. USACHCS mission is to educate and train Army Chaplain and Chaplain Assistants to provide spiritual, religious and moral leadership instruction during war and peace. Perhaps, self-care strategies are expected of the minister once they enter the chaplaincy? I suggest addressing the issues of self-care to identify, minimize, and perhaps to eliminate burnout and/or compassion fatigue during a chaplain's formative years. This suggestion can be applied during the Chaplain Officer Basic Course, which is an initial entry course to become a chaplain. Practicing self-care is a must for first term chaplains. A self-care model will help establish a foundation for self-care that can be enhanced as they mature in ministry and the chaplaincy. The chaplaincy needs to have in place varieties of policies, procedures and resources for preventing burnout and/or compassion fatigue and treating it when it occurs during a chaplain's years of active ministry.

The heavy demands on the chaplain from Global War On Terrorism (GWOT) have encouraged the Chaplain Corps to establish formal training courses to address the issue of compassion fatigue and burnout. The 22th Chief of Chaplains spoke on the subject of maintaining spiritual health, resiliency and vitality:

> "In an uncertain future of persistent conflict, I believe the greatest dangers we face as spiritual care givers are the 'the compassion fatigue' and ministry burn-out that can sap our ability to provide compassionate religious support to others. As spiritual leaders, we must ensure that we are all engaged both in self-care and group-care initiatives in order to maintain our own spirituality, religious fortitude, and faith.[33]

Currently, the Army Chaplaincy is experiencing low retention. Several factors contribute

---

[33] The Chief of Chaplain's Newsletter, (October 2007), 1.

to this dilemma: difficulties with supervisory chaplain, burnout and OPTEMPO.[34] Operating tempo (OPTEMPO) is the annual operating miles or hours for a piece of equipment. OPTEMPO is a tool used by commanders to forecast fuel and repair parts for training events in their units, thus establishing a training pace for the Soldiers. The Chaplain Corps is being intentional on prevention. In addition to the chaplain focusing on self-care techniques, perhaps the chaplain can take advantage of their endorsing agent's sabbatical program, retreat centers that exist or other techniques they offer. Due to the OPTEMPO some chaplains are opting, which otherwise would not, to apply for advanced civilian schooling. Advanced civilian schooling is perhaps an opportunity to attend an accredited school and earn an instructor billet which would greatly minimize the opportunities to deploy as frequent. Advanced civilian schooling allows the chaplain to specialize in a specific area of interest. Some areas of interest that can earn a masters degree are: world religions, ethics, Clinical Pastoral Education, family life, and resource management.

The advanced civilian schooling education time line is one to two years for schooling. The requirements are to fulfill a minimum three year utilization tour with other utilization requirements based on the needs of the Army. Once the chaplain receives their specialized training he or she can be called to return to their specialization. This amount of training can possibly take a chaplain away from the deployment cycle for four years or longer. The current deployment time in a combat theater is fifteen months. A normal combat tour is twelve months in theater.

The U.S. Army is a professional organization and chaplains are a part of this professional organization. The U.S. Army Chaplain Corps is a proud and honorable profession. Chaplains have a unique moral role in the Army, as does the church ministers. "No other professional is expected to model integrity as is a church minister."[35] This attitude of expectations is taken into the U.S. Army Chaplaincy. 'Building awareness' within the Army community of the phenomenon of clergy burnout and its causes is, obviously, a critical starting point. Chaplains themselves must possess such awareness and be able to convey it, but other leaders in the wider Army must be enlightened on this topic. The leaders who make and implement policy need to be abreast of the chaplain's dilemma.

The chaplain's technical and staff chain of command channels can set standards and articulate expectations regarding chaplain health and wholeness. Commanders and supervisory chaplains can and should insist that chaplains work at a sane humane pace-limiting hours worked per week to a realistic, agreed upon standard. Unfortunately, commanders, which consist of the staff chain of command, have unrealistic expectations

---

[34] Briefing to ILE Students at Ft. Belvoir, VA. by the OCCH Training Manager on Transformation in the Army Chaplain Corps, 20 February 2007.

[35] Joe E. Trull and James C. Carter, Ministerial Ethics. Being a Good Minister in a Not-So-Good World, (Nashville: Broadman, 1983), 59.

of the chaplain. They are required by the military to attend a pre-commanders course before taking command. During this course they receive instructions by senior chaplains on the duties and responsibilities of chaplains and chaplain assistants that will be assigned to their units. The commanders are instructed that the Unit Ministry Team (UMT) is a combat multiplier, a major advantage to their command team. There is no other staff element in the command that can substitute the duties of the UMT. Chaplains are that one person Soldiers can confide in. Chaplains are needed and are important! No one else is in a position to minister to Soldiers.

Regardless of these instructions, some commanders ignore reality and improperly use the chaplain. One reason for this ignorance is due to the commanders not being a part of the chaplain's religious worship services that take part on the weekends. Commanders often do not know or appreciate what chaplains do during worship times. By not visiting the chaplain during their worship services or other religious events that support the unit the commanders will draw a conclusion that the chaplain is not contributing to the command. Again, the awareness of the chaplain's role has been established through instruction, but the commander fails to acknowledge that the chaplain is an asset to the command team.

Chaplains should be expected to experience Sabbath rest on a regular basis: adequate rest each day, Sabbath time each week, annual holiday and vacation times, periodic sabbaticals. Many times these periodic sabbaticals manifest themselves in the chaplain attending their denominational conferences. It is almost impossible for the chaplain to take a one to three month sabbatical. The military annual leave system is not organized in that fashion.

The military leave policy consist of a Soldier earning two and a half days of leave each month, thus totaling thirty days of leave for the year. If a Soldier exceeds sixty days of leave within a year the military will take days away until the Soldier is under sixty days. The base line is sixty days. This process is called 'use or loss leave.'

Unlike civilian clergy and professional lay ministers the chaplain's lifestyle has no room for an entire sabbatical program. There is tremendous value in the holiness of a sabbatical program. Most sabbatical programs are formational and look to the continual growth and development of the human person in every aspect. A call to holiness is a call to wholeness. The ideal is that sabbatical programs are designed for spiritual refreshment, theological renewal, and where ministers can minister to one another. When is there time for the deploying chaplain to take advantage of a sabbatical program? Currently, the deployment cycle rotation in a combat theater is fifteen months. To find the time to participate in a three to four month long sabbatical program is unseen. Elements of a sabbatical program can be incorporated in the spiritual disciplines of a chaplain's life, but not without interruption. Some endorsing agents use their denominational conferences as mini sabbaticals.

Intra-Personal Factors

This section will look at some of the critical internal factors-traits and tendencies within the chaplain that contribute significantly to the reality of clergy burnout and/or compassion fatigue. One of the most obvious factors that can lead to burnout and/or compassion fatigue is neglecting our needs for maintaining bodily health—'diet, exercise, and rest.' Many times, emotional or relational problems have their roots in neglect of the physical body.[36] A host of studies show that physical activity can greatly reduce levels of stress.[37] Establishing a stress-less physical activity for chaplains can become challenging. It is ironic that the demanding physical activity of the US Army can add to the stress level of chaplains rather than assist. Chaplains are often expected to perform in physical training equally with Soldiers who are many years younger than the chaplain. So the physical training becomes an added stress factor rather than a benefit.

John Sanford identifies another intra-personal factor contributing to clergy burnout is the need of pastors functioning often on their 'persona.'[38] Mr. Sanford states that 'persona' is, the "front or mask we assume in order to meet and relate to the outer world, especially the world of other people.[39] The persona has a double function. One function is to help us project our personality out effectively into the world. The other function is to protect us from the outer world by enabling us to assume a certain outer posture but at the same time keep other aspects of ourselves hidden from other."[40] To have a persona is not, in and of itself, a bad thing. It is the abuse, not the use of the persona that can contribute to clergy burnout. For example, an introverted person whose job demands him or her to be extroverted can be draining. They must allow time to nurture their introverted side, which is their dominate side. A trusted friend, mentor or spiritual director could provide an invaluable assistance at this point.

A related factor that contributes to clergy burnout and/or compassion fatigue is the tendency to 'overfunction' in ministry. Family systems theory introduced this phase. It is critical for chaplains to understand this phenomenon of overfunctioning in themselves and to recognize that it is part of how they respond to anxiety. The late Edwin Friedman was a pioneer in applying insights from systems thinking to the "family" of the parish.

> One of the most universal complaints from clergy of all faiths is the feeling of being stuck with all the responsibility. (Compare Moses's complaints in Numbers 11:11ff.) This can extend from ideas for programming to turning out the lights in the office....What rarely occurs to those in the

---

[36] Donald D. Vickery and James F. Fries, <u>Take Care of Yourself</u>, (Massachusetts: Addison-Wesley Publishing Company, Inc., 1989), 28-30.

[37] Charles R. Swindoll, "Stress: Calm Answers for the Worry Worn" (Portland: Lockman Foundation, 1977), 13.

[38] Sanford, 11.

[39] Ibid, 11.

[40] Ibid, 14.

overfunctioning position is that in any type of family the rest of the system may be underfunctioning as an adaptive response![41]

Another issue is the 'reality of human sinfulness.' The Lutheran tradition employs the phrase *simul iustus et peccator* ("at the same time saint and sinner"). It illustrates that even sinners remain among the righteous within the church. Self-care would not be needed if sin did not exist. Sin exists not only in the people the chaplain ministers to, but sin resides in the chaplain as well. When the soul is not at rest, it is in a state of chaos. One particular manifestation of sin is the chaplain's neglect of his own spiritual life with God. "It is ironic that pastors who, in most cases, received their call to ministry through a particular worship experience or series of worship experiences should rarely have the opportunity to worship again," declares Charles Rassieur. "Instead, pastors are the priests who preside over the celebration of the rites and observations of a church....What was at one time sacred or holy can easily become commonplace for the pastor....Without a vibrant spiritual life, the pastor soon finds ministry to be too demanding for human resources alone."[42]

It is possible that scriptures are used to convey an unhealthy understanding of caring for one's self. The reading from "Our Daily Bread," 9 September 2003, is titled "Living with Grace" and is based on the scripture of 1 Peter 5:5-11. The author relates that instead of relating to others from a position of superiority, we must put others ahead of ourselves. We should wear the clothes of humility because He 'resists the proud, but gives grace to the humble," 1 Peter 5:5.[43] Humility is important. But always putting others ahead of ourselves leads to the dangerous area of burnout. The Bible is a road map that God has established so His people can understand His character better. If the Bible is read out of context, then it becomes a manipulative tool instead of a regenerative tool.

Chaplains juggle a number of balls at the same time: relationship with God, relationship with self, and if married relationships with spouse and family. Licensed marriage counselors, considering the issue of military deployments, state that six to eighteen months are needed for marriages to return to normalcy of the marriage prior to the deployment.[44] It is difficult to reach this mark with the frequent deployment rotations. The military has identified this dilemma and is trying to stabilize the Soldier and their family. Unfortunately the demands are high and often the Soldier is expected to function regularly immediately following the deployment. The demands of balancing work, caring for one's spiritual well-being, ministry and family concerns contribute to chaplains violating self-care and not depending on God.

---

[41] Edwin H. Friedman, Generation to Generation: Family Process in Church and Synagogue. New York and London: The Guilford Press, 1985), 211.

[42] Charles L. Rassieur, "Career Burnout Prevention Among Pastoral Counselors and Pastors": In Handbook for Basic Types of Pastoral Care and Counseling, ed. Howard W. Stone and William M. Clements, (Nashville: Abingdon, 1991), 262-263.

[43] RBC Ministries, Our Daily Bread (2003).

[44] Unit Ministry Team Training, "Deployment Cycle," Fort Hood, Texas, October 2004.

Uniqueness of Military Ministry

Chaplains are always present with their Soldiers in war and peace, but the uniqueness of a chaplain in comparison to other care givers is that chaplains deploy. Chaplains deploy to war with Soldiers as they go in harm's way, thus placing their lives at risk. The U.S. Army Chief of Chaplains has a policy that states 'any deploying unit will deploy with a Unit Ministry Team (UMT), particularly a chaplain.[45] The UMT's main mission is to provide the free exercise of religion for the military personnel. Chaplains deploy to perform and provide religious support to the sons and daughters of America.

Currently, the nation's security has been in turmoil, but was heighten after 9-11. For example, the trail of terror started on February 26, 1993, with the first World Trade Center bombing. On June 26, 1996, the Khobar Towers in Saudi Arabia were bombed; 19 Americans killed, hundreds of others wounded. On August 7, 1998, truck bombings of U.S. embassies in Kenya and Tanzania killed more than 250 people. On October 12, 2000, suicide bombers attacked the USS Cole in Aden, Yemen, killing 17 sailors. On September 11, 2001, hijacked jets flew into the World Trade Center, Pentagon, and a field in Pennsylvania. Nearly 3,000 people were killed during 9-11.

To date, the military is fighting wars in Iraq and Afghanistan, reinforcing political relationships in Liberia, Haiti, and Djibouti Africa, preparing for contingencies in North Korea and Iran, supporting peacekeeping operations in Bosnia, Kosovo, and Sinai. With the nation's security at stake, the armed services, particular the Army plays a major role. Deploying to war is the rule and not the exception anymore. When units deploy, Soldiers deploy, and when Soldiers deploy, chaplains deploy. The Army Chief of Chaplain's policy states that every deploying unit will include a chaplain and a chaplain assistant. The responsibility of the UMT is to ensure the Soldiers free exercise of religion is not violated. This allows the Soldier to exercise their religious convictions. The question is not will the chaplain be affected by the ugliness of war, but by how much will the chaplain be affected? Chaplains are placed in traumatic situations to provide and perform ministry and will be affected in some fashion. The above listed examples illustrate some of the situational factors unique to the culture of the U.S. Army.

Israel Drazin and Cecil B. Currey spoke about the uniqueness of the chaplaincy as they addressed an argument by two seniors at Harvard Law School in 1979:

> The decision spoke of the "mobile, deployable nature" of the military, the special and serious stresses encountered by its members, the separation, loneliness, strange surroundings, fears, financial hardships, and family problems faced by soldiers. In providing chaplains, "the Army has proceeded

---

[45] U.S. Army Chief of Chaplains, The U.S. Army Chaplaincy Strategic Plan FY 2008-2013, (Washington, D.C.: Government Printing Office, March, 2007).

on the premise that having uprooted the soldiers from their natural habitats it owes them a duty to satisfy their Free Exercise rights, especially since the failure to do so would diminish morale, thereby weakening our national defense.[46]

Another part of the chaplain's unique role is their ministry of presence. Ministry of presence is described when the chaplain is visible and makes themselves assessable for ministry opportunities. Chaplains present this ministry of presence on a daily basis, in war, during peace, births, deaths, hospital visits, weddings, and during traumatic situations. The chaplain is the symbolic representation of God and a caring community. The chaplain is a pastor to hospital patients, medical staff and families. He or she can provide sacraments and spiritual direction, which will help people focus on their own spiritual strengths. The chaplain is an advocate for the hospitalized patient, medical staff and family. The chaplain brings calmness in the midst of crisis. The chaplain can bring order out of chaos. The chaplain is the tangible evidence that someone cares. The chaplain is the facilitator with a human touch.

Both church attendees and non-church attendees may believe that the life of a pastor is an easy one. A perceived view holds that pastors serve a few hours a week in preparation for worship and then lead that worship time.

An article by Zig Ziglar counteracts this believe of clergy indolence by providing insight into a pastor's work schedule.

> "Reality gives us an entirely different picture. According to a study recently published in Leadership Journal, the average evangelical clergyman works 55 hours a week, including four evenings, and will also take average of four phone calls at home every night. As a result, sometime during the month, a typical pastor will feel both physical and emotional stress, and 42 percent of their spouses will complain about the schedule at least once a month.
>
> Most pastors work excessive hours voluntarily. It's not demanded by their boards or the congregations. They spend about 14 hours each week planning and attending meetings and services, 13 hours teaching and preparing sermons, nine hours in pastoral care and counseling, six hours in prayer and personal devotions and 13 hours in other tasks, which include long-range planning and evangelism. That leaves them precious little time for rejuvenation and recreation or time with the family and taking care of their own physical, mental, emotional and spiritual needs.

---

[46] Israel Drazin and Cecil B. Currey, FOR GOD AND COUNTRY: The History of a Constitutional Challenge to the Army Chaplaincy, (KTAV Publishing House, Inc., Hoboken, New Jersey, 1995), 198.

The results speak for themselves. The dropout rate is high. The number who suffer from fatigue, depression and other problems is higher than average in the population.

What's the message? Remember my pastor friend, that you can better serve your God, your family and your church by first taking care of some of your own needs. You've got to have energy to give it; you've got to have strength to share it. You've got to have the right spirit to convey it to others.

THIS IS not a selfish approach. It's a wise approach, and it will give you something to smile about."[47]

For the chaplain there is a personal cost of providing ministry in a military setting. When Abram received his divine calling from God (Genesis 12:1-9) there were great demands and many sacrifices attached with it. Chaplains, like Abram, have heard the call of God on their lives. They have committed themselves to ministry. They illustrate servant leadership. This sacrificial lifestyle has called them to leave their homes and communities, places of worship, their family and friends to go where God, and the Army, sends them. To maintain a productive state of spiritual well-being is a must, regardless of dangers and personal hardships, which may result in compassion fatigue and burnout. The chaplain is not immune to being spiritually depleted than they are immune from physical disease. The chaplain may have tremendous spiritual resources, but they are still affected by the shocking results of carelessness. When God called Abram, He mentioned that He would make Abram into a great nation and bless him (Genesis 12:2). God will honor the chaplain's personal commitment to holiness and their sacrificial service to God and country.

---

[47] Article by Zig Ziglar, Creators Syndicate, "Slow Down Preacher." 1993.

CHAPTER THREE

THEOLOGICAL AND SCRIPTURAL FRAMEWORK

Introduction

John P. Burgess states in his book, "Why Scripture Matters," that Scripture are a compelling power in the time of church conflict.[48] He questions why scriptures are not presently valued. Mr. Burgess writes that scripture has been a source of personal renewal.[49] We claim to honor scripture yet we ignore it. "We resolve to plumb the depths of scripture but seem, inevitably, to lack the patience and discipline. We claim that scripture is our book but too often conclude that it belongs to another time and place."[50]

Old Testament Foundation

Are chaplains violating scripture by not enforcing a Sabbath day and Lord's Day of rest? The fourth commandment in the Ten Commandments outlined in Exodus 20:9-11 and Deuteronomy 5:13-15 reads:

> "Remember the Sabbath day by keeping it holy. Six days you shall labor and do all your work, but the seventh day is a Sabbath to the Lord your God. On it you shall not do any work, neither you, nor your son or daughter, nor your manservant or maidservant, nor your animals, nor the alien within your gates. For in six days the Lord made the heavens and the earth, the sea, and

---

[48] John P. Burgess, <u>Why Scripture Matters: Reading the Bible in a Time of Church Conflict</u>, (Louisville: Westminster John Knox, 1998), 1-8.

[49] Burgess, 19.

[50] Ibid, 21.

all that is in them, but he rested on the seventh day. Therefore the Lord blessed the Sabbath day and made it holy."[51]

"Six days you shall labor and do all your work, but the seventh day is a Sabbath to the Lord your God. On it you shall not do any work, neither you, nor your son or daughter, nor your manservant or maidservant, nor your ox, your donkey or any of your animals, nor the alien within your gates, so nor your manservant or maidservant may rest, as you do. Remember that you were slaves in Egypt and that the Lord your God brought you out of there with a mighty hand and an outstretched arm. Therefore the Lord your God has commanded you to observe the Sabbath day."[52]

Regarding the aspect of Sabbath rest, Eugene Peterson writes:

An accurate understanding of Sabbath is prerequisite to its practice: it must be understood biblically, not culturally...Sabbath is not a day off and it is inexcusable that pastors, learned in Scripture and guardians of the sacred practices, should so misname it...Sabbath means quit. Stop. Take a break. Cool it...It is a word about time, denoting our nonuse of it, what we usually call *wasting* time...Sabbath-keeping often feels like an interruption, an interference with our routines. It challenges assumptions we gradually build up that our daily work is indispensable in making the world go."[53]

The fourth commandment requires of a person, a due portion of his time dedicated to the worship and service of God.

The fourth commandment (Exodus 20:8-11) reads;

"Remember the Sabbath day by keeping it holy. Six days you shall labor and do all your work, but the seventh day is a Sabbath to the Lord your God. On it you shall not do any work, neither you, nor your son or daughter, nor your manservant or maidservant, nor your animals, nor the alien within your gates. For in six days the Lord made the heavens and the earth, the sea, and all that is in them, but he rested on the seventh day. Therefore the Lord blessed the Sabbath day and made it holy.

The fourth commandment addresses the period of worship while giving specific instructions regarding the use of time. Time is a gift from God and should be given back to God and used for Him. The fourth commandment also addresses God's people maintaining their physical and spiritual strength, thus establishing a foundation for self-care.

---

[51] Exodus 20:8-11, NIV.

[52] Deuteronomy 5:13-15, NIV.

[53] Eugene H. Peterson, <u>Working the Angles: The Shape of Pastoral Integrity.</u> (Grand Rapids: Eerdmans, 1987), 66-70.

The fourth commandment, the first of two positive commands in the Decalogue, highlights the rhythm work and rest, which can serve as a guiding principle for authentic self-care.[54] The fourth commandment can be viewed in two parts: first, the command (Exodus 20:8; Deuteronomy 5:12) and second, the instructions on how to execute the command (Exodus 20:9-11; Deuteronomy 5:13-15). The Decalogue in Exodus chapter twenty was spoken by God to Moses and Moses repeats the Decalogue forty years later in Deuteronomy chapter five to the nation of Israel. The Exodus explanation centers the nation of Israel's attention upon God the Creator and was commanded to keep the Sabbath because God keep it. The Deuteronomy explanation centered Israel's attention upon humans. They were commanded to keep the Sabbath as a reminder of their ancestors being slaves in Egypt and toiling for four hundred years without a day of rest.

Israel was God's chosen nation and the Sabbath was given to them to distinguish them from other nations. The Sabbath observance highlighted Israel's uniqueness among the nations. Keeping the Sabbath was unknown to other nations. The Sabbath was given as a sign of the Mosaic Covenant (Exodus 31:12-18). A covenant sign was a visible reminder of covenant commitments. The rainbow would be the sign of the Noahic Covenant (Genesis 9:13) and circumcision would be the sign of the Abrahamic Covenant (Genesis 17:11).[55]

Sabbath is derived from a Hebrew word meaning "to cease, abstain, or desist." It refers to the last day of a seven day week which, in the Jewish religion, is a day on which one rests from his normal activity, devoting himself to the service of God. The observance of the Sabbath was one of the Ten Commandments and is traced back to God ceasing work on the seventh day of his creation activity. To observe the Sabbath implies action. Faith is never passive-always active. To remember the Sabbath day by ceasing from work to contemplate God's creative work in the world and God's involvement with Israel's liberation out of Egypt is intentional action.[56] Breaking of the Sabbath by performance of proscribed labor, was punishable by death (Exodus 31:14; Numbers 15: 32-36).

God 'ceased' from his labors for two reasons: First, God ceased from His creative work because His work of creation was complete (Genesis 2:1; Exodus 31:17). God needed no rest because He had not grown weary from His six days of creation work. The prophet Isaiah speaks:

> Do you not know? Have you not heard? The Lord is the everlasting God,
> the Creator of the ends of the earth. He will not grow tired or weary, and
> His understanding no one can fathom (Isaiah 40:28).

---

[54] Partial fulfillment of the requirements for Unit 4, Clinical Pastoral Education Pastoral Project, by Richard G. Anderson at Walter Reed Army Medical Center, 2004.

[55] Arnold G. Fruchtenbaum, "Israelology: Part 1 of 6," Chafer Theological Seminary Journal, 1999, 41-49.

[56] Matthew Henry's Commentary On the Whole Bible: Genesis to Deuteronomy, Volume 1. (Peabody: Hendrickson Publisher's, 1992), 318-320.

Secondly, God ceased from His labors as an illustration of the eternal rest He would provide for His people. The rest God received in Genesis 2:1-3 is a promise of the continual rest that He would and did provide through the second Adam, Jesus Christ. Hebrews 4: 1-10 is a testament of God's promise and pattern of eternal rest established for believers.

> Therefore, since the promise of entering his rest still stands, let us be careful that none of you be found to have fallen short of it. For we also have had the gospel preached to us, just as they did; but the message they heard was of no value to them, because those who heard did not combine it with faith. Now we who have believed enter that rest, just as God has said, "So I declared on oath in my anger, They shall never enter my rest." And yet his work has been finished since the creation of the world. For somewhere he has spoken about the seventh day in these words: "And on the seventh day God rested from all his work." And again in the passage above he says, "They shall never enter my rest." It still remains that some will enter that rest, and those who formerly had the gospel preached to them did not go in, because of their disobedience. Therefore God again set a certain day, calling it Today, when a long time later he spoke through David, as was said before: "Today, if you hear his voice, do not harden your hearts." For if Joshua had given them rest, God would not have spoken later about another day. There remains, then, a Sabbath-rest for the people of God; for anyone who enters God's rest also rests from his own work, just as God did from his.

Sabbath translated from Hebrew is 'shabbat' (Genesis 2:1-3), which means to cease, desist, the weekly day of rest and abstention from work.[57] The word Sabbath is not used here (Genesis 2:1-3) but seventh is, thus equating the two. The first record of Sabbath observance is when the whole Israelite community escaped from Egypt to Sinai (Exodus 16:25-30). The fourth commandment simply requires the nation of Israel to labor for six days and to observe a day of sacred rest. This establishes a structure and pace to work and rest; six days of labor followed by a day of rest.

New Testament Interpretation

By the time of Jesus' ministry, Sabbath-keeping was regarded as one of the distinctive features of Jewish religion, and proper observance had developed into a highly technical affair, with ingenious methods of avoiding certain regulations. The true spirit and purpose of the Sabbath, however, had been obscured. When Jesus plucked grain for food (Matthew

---

[57] Paul J. Achtemeier, "Harper's Bible Dictionary" San Francisco: Harper Collins, 1985), 888.

12:1-8) or healed on the Sabbath (Matthew 12:9-14), the Pharisees who were the religious legalist, reacted violently and charged Jesus with doing what was not lawful to do on the Sabbath. In Matthew 12:1-8, Jesus permitted the disciples actions of picking and eating grain from a field on the Sabbath. The reality was the disciples were not working on the Sabbath day, which was prohibited by the Mosaic Law (Exodus 34:21), but they were satisfying their hunger. Simply satisfying their hunger was allowed according to the stipulation in Deuteronomy 23:24-25.

Jesus responds to the Pharisee's legalistic allegation with three illustrations; first, David's preservation of his own life (Matthew 12:3-4), second, the priests ministering on the Sabbath day in the temple (Matthew 12:5), and lastly, Jesus' stance that He is the Lord of the Sabbath day (Matthew 12:6-8). His answers showed them the Sabbath had not been given to test their obedience or ingenuity, but to assist them in maintaining their physical and spiritual strength. His actions were in fact a fulfillment of God's original purpose in giving the Sabbath. As the Lord of the Sabbath, Jesus, the Son of God, shared in giving the original Sabbath law to Israel in the first place.[58]

Paul's epistle to the Colossians was written to oppose certain cults and to tell how faith in Christ is complete. Nothing needs to be added to what Christ did. The Sabbath is the only directive in the Decalogue not to be observed in the New Testament. Colossians 2:14-17 reads:

> Having cancelled the written code, with its regulations, that was against us and that stood opposed to us; he took it away, nailing it to the cross. And having disarmed the powers and authorities, he made a public spectacle of them, triumphing over them by the cross. Therefore do not let anyone judge you by what you eat or drink, or with regard to a religious festival, a New Moon celebration or a Sabbath day.

As stated earlier, the Sabbath command functioned as a sign of the Mosaic Covenant (Exodus 31:12-18). When the Mosaic Covenant ended, the Sabbath command ended. Under the New Testament, dispensation of grace, the Old Testament concept of Sabbath obedience is obsolete. Gentile Christians were not instructed to keep and observe the Sabbath. The author of Acts writes:

> Instead we should write to them, telling them to abstain from sexual immorality, from the meat of strangled animals and from blood. You are to abstain from food sacrificed to idols, from blood, from the meat of strangled animals and from sexual immorality. You will do well to avoid these things (Acts 15:20, 29).

---

[58] Arthur L. Farstad, "We Believe: Jesus Is Lord," Journal of the Grace Evangelical Society 2 (Spring 1989), 5.

Colossians 2:13-17, shows a progression of thought referencing subjects such as; Old Testament dietary laws, festivals, sacrifices, and the Sabbath day were not intended to be practiced forever.[59] Paul is not condemning these Old Testament practices, but his intent is to show that Christians are free from the demands of the Mosaic Law. In verse 17, Paul uses the term, *shadow of things to come*; he is suggesting the temporary nature of the Old Testament practices.[60] He is revealing the shadowy nature of the Mosaic Law. When Jesus Christ, the Lord of the Sabbath, appeared on the scene the Sabbath day, which was given as a sign of the Mosaic Covenant cease to exist (Exodus 31:12-18). Jesus Christ the Lord of the Sabbath fulfilled the Sabbath.

The Lord's Day literally means, the day belongs to the Lord. The phrase, Lord's Day, occurs only once in the New Testament. Revelation 1:10 reads, "On the Lord's Day I was in the Spirit, and I heard behind me a loud voice like a trumpet." There are several scriptures that make it clear that it was the first day of the week, or Sunday (Mark 16: 9; John 20: 19; Acts 20: 7; 1 Corinthians 16: 2; Matthew 28: 1, 5, 6, and 9). This being the first day of the week in the Christian order commemorates the new creation with Christ Himself as its resurrected head. It is not a mere changeover from the Sabbath but a new day marking a new dispensation.[61] This dispensation is one of grace, not the law.

The phrase, the Lord's Day, occurs in early Christian literature as the first day of the week. A similar phrase appears in *The Teaching of the Twelve Apostles*, also known as the *Didache* (Gk., "teaching"), a work written toward the end of the first century, probably in Syria.[62] The principle of dedicating one day out of seven to God (Mosaic Covenant) is present in the Gospel believer's practice. William Barclay comments:

> There is no doubt at all that from the early second century onwards - and perhaps even earlier – the Lord's Day has completely displaced the Sabbath, and that the two are never confused, and are even contrasted with each other.[63]

Even though the Sabbath is replaced by the Lord's Day, certain principles are still applicable to contemporary times understanding of biblical self-care. For example, the issues of time, the pace of work and rest, and the death penalty for violating the Sabbath. For Gospel believers the punishment is not a literal death, but perhaps death to one's ministry due to failing health, compassion fatigue and burnout. People become unbalanced and fragmented when they are out of sync or off beat with God's rhythm of work and rest. God is interested in the whole person, both physically and spiritually, and how we best use

---

[59] Matthew Henry's Commentary On the Whole Bible: Acts to Revelation, Volume 6. (Peabody: Hendrickson Publisher's, 1992), 611.

[60] Ibid, 611-613.

[61] Merrill F. Unger, The New Unger's Bible Dictionary, (Moody Press: Chicago, 1988), 782.

[62] Achtemeier, 574.

[63] William Barclay, The Ten Commandments. 2d ed., (Louisville: Westminster John Knox Press, 1998), 21.

our time for self nurture.[64] Time is a precious commodity, it is sacred. It is a gift from God and should be used wisely. In his letter to the Ephesians, the Apostle Paul writes:

> Be very careful, then, how you live – not as unwise but as wise, making the most of every opportunity, because the days are evil. Therefore, do not be foolish, but understand what the Lord's will is (Ephesians 5:15-17; cp. Colossians 4:5).

To use this gift of time wisely calls for some structure or a set pace. The structure or pace was established with the Sabbath day: work and rest. The New Testament scriptures address the aspect of hard work and condemns being idle or lazy (Acts 20: 33-35; 2 Thessalonians 3: 10 and 13). Paul is setting the example of hard work versus coveting, the willingness to work versus being able to work, but not wanting to work.

Viewed in this light, the structure of work and rest sets one in pace with God's concern of his *imago dei*, people shaped in His image (Genesis 1:26). God is concerned about the physical and spiritual life of the whole person, the wellbeing of humanity. This biblical self-care uses God's time wisely and focuses God's people to worship Him for His creative work which was celebrated on the Sabbath day and His redemptive work which was celebrated on the Lord's Day. Paul's first pastoral letter to Timothy addresses the practice of spiritual disciplines to grow in godliness. The Apostle Paul writes:

> Having nothing to do with godless myths and old wives' tales, rather, train yourself to be godly. For physical training is of some value, but godliness has value for all things, holding promise for both the present life and the life to come (1 Timothy 4:7-8).

Spiritual disciplines are the thought and behavior patterns that draw us away from an improper focus on ourselves and the world to a proper focus on God and on His word.[65] Some of the spiritual disciplines are prayer, confession, meditation, fellowship, evangelism, worship, fasting, solitude, submission, simplicity, accountability, and stewardship.[66]

The president of the United States, the military's Commander in Chief, George W. Bush, finds strength in spiritual disciplines. President Bush begins each morning with the discipline of daily devotions, a practice he began in Community Bible Study in Midland, Texas. His devotions consist of reading a section from *My Utmost for His Highest* by Oswald Chambers, reading his favorite Old Testament scriptures, Psalms 27 and 91,

---

[64] H. Beecher Hicks, Jr. Preaching Through A Storm. (Grand Rapids, Michigan: Zondervan Publishing House. 1987), 61-68.

[65] Stephen Eyre, The Disciples Series: Spiritual Disciplines. (Grand Rapids, Michigan: Zondervan Publishing House, 1992), 9.

[66] Donald S. Whitney, Spiritual Disciplines for the Christian Life. (Colorado Springs: NavPress, 1991), 25-40.

meditation and prayer.[67] He has carried these spiritual disciplines with him to his position as the U.S. American president.

A comparison and contrast can show that the Old Testament Sabbath day was given to the Nation of Israel (Exodus 31: 12-17) and the New Testament Lord's Day was given to Gospel believers (John 20: 19-25). The Sabbath day was observed on the seventh day of the week (Exodus 20: 10) and the Lord's Day was observed on the first day of the week. The Sabbath day celebrated God's work of creation (Exodus 20: 11) and the Lord's Day celebrated God's work of redemption (Matthew 28: 1-7).[68]

The Lord's Day is reference to Christ resurrection and dispensation of grace. The Sabbath was under the Mosaic Law and for Israel only. Jesus calls himself the Lord of the Sabbath. So, on the Lord's Day, we are to cease from working and contemplate God's creative work and the resurrection, thus getting into a pace of work and rest.

Jesus Modeling Self-Care

Jesus balanced his life by caring for Himself so that he could provide pastoral care for others. Matthew 14:13-36 (vs. 13, 22-25) provides understanding for this point. The setting takes place in Nazareth, a town in Galilee, which is on the west side of the Sea of Galilee. Nazareth is the hometown of Jesus. Jesus and the disciples have had a full and exciting day of preaching and teaching the Gospel to many people. During this period, Herod the tetrarch beheads John the Baptist. When Jesus heard what had happen to John the Baptist He withdrew by boat privately to a solitary place. The death of John the Baptist must have taken a toll on Jesus. With the lost of his dear friend and relative Jesus experienced strong emotions of anger and grief. After all, the two had a wonderful relationship. Luke 1: 34-36 tells of the angel foretelling of the birth of Jesus to the Virgin Mary. The angel tells Mary that her relative, Elizabeth, the mother of John the Baptist, is expecting a child even in her old age. In addition to them being related John the Baptist prepares the way for Jesus and baptizes Jesus (Matthew 3: 1-17). In addition to Jesus mourning his relatives death He perhaps saw the parallel to His death. "Like John, Jesus will incur the displeasure of this world's political leaders and will be executed."[69]

Jesus' actions; withdrawing by boat privately to a solitary place, illustrates one of his self-care techniques. Matthew 14:13 reads, *"When Jesus heard what had happened, he withdrew by boat privately to a solitary place."*[70] Jesus withdrawing by boat alone to a secluded place was an intentional act to separate himself from the crowds of people. Jesus

---

[67] Stephen Mansfield, <u>The Faith of George W. Bush.</u> (New York, NY: Penguin Group, 2003), 119-120.

[68] John F. Walvoord and Roy B. Zuck. <u>The Bible Knowledge Commentary: New Testament.</u> (Colorado Springs: Victor, 2000), 92-93.

[69] Douglas R.A. Hare, Interpretation of Matthew: A Bible Commentary for Teaching and Preaching. (Louisville: John Knox Press, 1993), 165.

[70] Matthew 14:13, NIV.

realized his physical, emotional, mental and spiritual limitations. During this moment Jesus located a non-public place so he could be alone. Jesus was not bound by performance doing. Jesus had being - worth. It is for you to be; it is for God to do, provides a simple but wise piece of advice.[71] "One of the greatest days of our lives is the day we first feel a joyous sensation about who we are simply because we are."[72] God is excited about who we are and the care giver can share in the joy of being called a child of God.

Regarding the aspect of being, Eugene Peterson writes:

> If God sets apart one day to rest, we can too. There are some things that can be accomplished, even by God, only in a state of rest…The precedent to quit doing and simply *be* is divine.[73]

We have an infinite void in our hearts that we attempt to fill with noise, people, busy-ness, possessions, and other finite things.[74] This is a major sickness in our culture. We are addicted to noise. We need noise. We've got to have noise! Silence is creepy, even frightening. Noise helps us live on the banks of denial. Noise keeps us concentrated on something else-anything else!

We are addicted to company. Notice also the many ways we work to fill the space around us. We fear being alone. We fear solitude. It is this fear that reveals a desperate insecurity within us. However, our attempts to fill our lives with company will never satisfy the true hunger of the heart-community with God. I am not suggesting that we do not need relationships with other people. On the contrary, we need more true relationships with other people. However, time is necessary if one is to develop a true friendship with God. This must be time spent in solitude.

Solitude is the practice of being absent from other people and other things so that you can be present with God. In solitude, we rest from our attempts to re-create the world in our image. We rest from arranging our relationships and manipulating people with our words. In solitude, we say to God, "I am here to be changed into whatever you like." In solitude, we learn to "wait on the Lord."

Solitude teaches us to hear the voice of God, since we are cut off from the hundreds of other voices that call out to us from our usual company.[75] Solitude forces us to face despair, yet it provides the only opportunity to discover the amazing power of God's presence. Too often, we run from our loneliness. It is only here in our lonely experiences that we truly comprehend the words of Jesus, "I am with you always, even to the end of the ages."

---

[71] Walter A. Henrichsen, Disciples are Made not Born: How to help others grow to maturity in Christ, (Colorado Springs, CO: Cook Communication Ministries, 1988), 121.

[72] Jones, 108.

[73] Eugene, 70.

[74] Didactic taught by William V. Arnold, Ph.D, "The Whole Person and Pastoral Care." Walter Reed Army Medical Center, Washington, D.C., 9 December 2003.

[75] Jones, 75-81.

Silence is the practice of quieting every voice, including your own inner and outer voices. Silence means being still, so that we can hear the voice that searches our hearts and minds.[76] We must quiet our own hearts and mouths if we are to be able to listen to the voice of God.

Silence also means excusing ourselves from the voices of others.[77] The demands of the world around us do not easily go away. We hear countless requests and demands each day over the radio, on the television, via email, telephonic devices and from the people around us. Each vying for our time and attention. Certainly some of these voices are important for us to hear, especially the voices of our family. However, there is One Voice that is, above all, necessary for us to hear. For this reason, we must develop habits of being unavailable to the voices all around us so we can learn to hear the Divine Voice.

Silence is also necessary to free ourselves from our tendency to control. Silence frees us from the tyranny we hold over others with our words. It is not speaking that breaks our silence, but the anxiety to be heard.[78] When we are silent, it is much more difficult to manipulate and control the people and circumstances around us. Words are the weapons we lay down when we practice silence. We give up our insistence of being heard and obeyed. Silence forces us to surrender to the will of God.

Solitude and silence, combined with an engaged mind; these are the practices to open our lives up to the grace of God. God says, "Be still, and know that I am God" (Psalm 46:10). This combination is the practice of waiting on the Lord. It is active stillness. This is the readying of one's heart to receive.

After this self-care moment, Jesus recharged and better able to minister, fed five thousand people by multiplying five loaves of bread and two fish. Jesus instructed the disciples to go on ahead of him and he dismissed the crowd. (v. 22) Matthew 14: 23 and 25a, *"After he dismissed them, he went up on a mountainside by himself to pray. When evening came, he was alone, during the fourth watch of the night."* Jesus sent the disciples and the crowds away with one purpose in mind. That purpose was to be by himself to pray. Jesus then modeled that private prayer and not corporate worship are greatly needed in our lives. Jesus was on the mountain from evening to the fourth watch of the night (3 a.m. to 6 a.m.) until he decided to visit the disciples on the lake. Being on a mountain gives one a bigger view of the terrain. Symbolically, one can gain a wider picture of self and their circumstances. God has the best interest of the care giver in mind. During this intimate time of fellowship, the chaplain is in the presence of God. Being in the presence of God gives one peace and assurance in the mist of chaos. When the chaplain is in fellowship with God he or she can verbalize their story to God. Only God can be 'fully' trusted with the chaplain's innermost feelings and thoughts. This is extremely important, especially in combat situations, when the sights and sounds of combat become overwhelming. I think

---

[76] Jones, 104.
[77] Ibid, 83-92.
[78] Ibid, 83.

this is equally important when chaplains depart each duty assignment. Chaplains can be assigned to any duty installation ranging from six months to six years. This type of nomadic life resembles the journeys of the Israelites, Jesus and His disciples. When Jesus' disciples would return from a strenuous preaching mission, their Master recognized their need for rest and invited them to come with Him to a quiet place where they could be refreshed (Mark 6:31).

In each illustration of Jesus conducting self-care several traits stand out. First, Jesus was intentional about conducting self-care. Jesus practiced self-awareness; He was aware of His emotional status. Jesus knew the importance of caring for himself and that the downside of self-care is self-neglect. Second, Jesus also knew the importance of being alone. Third, Jesus located secluded peaceful localities. Finally, Jesus had a scheduled time blocked out for self-care, self-examination, and prayer. This is a period of addressing one's emotional, physical, spiritual, and psychological limitations. Jesus prayed, as a reminder, that God is in control. This is illustrated when Jesus was alone in prayer from 3 a.m. to 6 a.m. Many times, this simple principle is forgotten during the stress and persecution of life. For the Christian Chaplain remembering that God is in control comes in learning and remembering to trust in Jesus Christ during the midst of stress and persecution.

Conclusion

Conducting self-care is simply challenging! The difficulty increases when conducted in a military environment: peace or combat for the above stated reasons. Conducting self-care is not impossible, but requires innovation. Jesus Christ offered the self-care model of intentionality, being alone (never alone, but alone with God), in a secluded quiet place, with a scheduled block of time, and relying on the power of prayer. As illustrated in the pericope, Jesus was able to conduct self-care during a turbulent moment in his life: not being accepted in his home town, mourning the death of John the Baptist and providing pastoral care on three separate occasions. Ministry is both demanding and rewarding. Conducting self-care will help chaplains survive the demands of ministry, to enjoy the rewards and benefits from the blessings. God is not asking the chaplains to live perfectly as Jesus did, but God wants the chaplains to live holy as Jesus did.

CHAPTER FOUR

METHODOLOGY

Introduction

I took a critical thinking approach when I started gathering my thoughts toward a thesis for a Doctor of Ministry. I wanted to have something of value that would benefit the U.S. Army Chaplain Corps and clergy in general. The Chaplain Corps includes the chaplains, chaplain assistants, staff, volunteers, directors of religious education, and lay ministers. My personal struggles were a part of the thinking process. I also considered how my experiences related to other chaplains and civilian pastors. What are some of our similarities? I thought about balance, health, and spiritual disciplines. What do they look like in a ministerial setting, particularly a military setting? What are their enemies? During that time that those questions came to mind I was recovering from burnout. Ultimately I asked myself, "What does it take to maintain spiritual strength in military ministry?" Much talk centers around physical care, but what about the spiritual self-care? I was using explorative research to identify whether there is a need for a model of self-care in the U.S. Army Chaplain Corps.

Research Design: Multiple Methods

During my time as a Clinical Pastoral Education (CPE) student at Walter Reed Army Medical Center (WRAMC), 2003-2004, two cohort groups were established to consider the research direction for the dissertation. On two separate occasions I presented to the groups a creative synthesis to help formulate my thoughts. Chaplains also volunteered to read my manuscript. The cohort groups and volunteers helped me frame my thoughts and think critically about my approach to research. I choose to develop my own model for the research rather than using an existing model. I wanted to establish my own independent critical thought process.

During my year of training at WRAMC, I traveled to Oblate School of Theology for academic class work on two separate occasions. A focus group was created at the school. The focus groups helped to generate questions and analytical ideas. Some of these questions included: What types of research methods, testing and data collection tools would I use. Also this group helped me consider the use of multiple research tools to include journal entries, field notes, interviews, a research dairy, verbatims and questionnaires. Initially, I used the multiple research methods. All of the research methods were helpful, but I chose to use field notes, interviews, and questionnaires. The use of field notes proved problematic. I could not change the form of how these notes were recorded. That was the only access I had. I would take field notes from didactics while at WRAMC, Oblate School of Theology, during monthly UMT training and other continuing education opportunities. Sometimes I was unable to get a recorded copy of the session, so I was left relying on my notes. Despite this downside the field notes still provided value.

My next method consisted of in-depth interviews which generated data from the participants. The interview process allowed candid comments by the speakers. The pool of chaplains interviewed included chaplains from active duty, reserve and National Guard and retired chaplains. In this same pool of chaplains I also used questionnaires. I combined the two techniques and conduct an interview schedule. This allowed the recipient to both complete a questionnaire and respond to clarifying questions by the interviewer.

The next method used was questionnaires with open-ended questions. This source provided excellent quantitative data. The questionnaires were distributed to the individuals and not to focus groups. The open-ended questions allowed for extended and more thoughtful responses from the respondents. The questionnaires were used to gather target data in responses to specific questions. I was able to gather enough data from the questions answered on the forms to make my own assessment. One challenge with questionnaires is collection of the forms. I successfully collected more questionnaires during the pre-test than during the pastoral research phase. During the pre-test I collected nine out of nine. For the pastoral research project I collected twenty-six out of twenty-nine.

Pre-Test Questionnaires

I conducted a field-test with my questionnaires and informal interviews with a senior group of military chaplains in order to surface and eliminate poorly constructed sentences and questions. The senior group of chaplains consisted of lieutenant colonel (0-5), colonel (0-6), and major general (0-8). They advised me to re-word some of the questions and statements. This pool of chaplains consisted of active component (active duty), reserve component (Reserve and National Guard), and retired U.S. Army Chaplains. These chaplains represented the full range of chaplain components. Often during the interviews, I felt I was listening to history being spoken, in particular with the 0-8 chaplains. My agenda was to have an unstructured interview with the senior chaplains. I wanted to gain as much wisdom as I possibly could. Most of the unstructured conversations were with the major generals.

The pre-test addressed the need for a self-care model in the U.S. Army Chaplain Corps. The Covenant and the Code of Ethics for Chaplains of the Armed Forces and the U.S. Army Chaplaincy Strategic Campaign Plan, FY 2000-2005 and 2008-2013 are guidelines and implies that the chaplain is conducting self-renewal. The intent with both directives is to focus on developing a deeper spiritual life in the U.S. Army Chaplaincy. The Chaplaincy Strategic Campaign Plan, 2008-2013 was enhanced from the U.S. Army Chaplaincy Strategic Campaign Plan, 2000-2005 to meet the needs of the U.S. Army as its transforms to meet the needs of the nation.

I administered a pre-test questionnaire (Appendix A: Pre-Test Questionnaire) to nine chaplains. Their rank ranged from captain, lieutenant colonel, and colonel. There were five captains that took the pre-test questionnaire. One of the captains was an Air Force Chaplain, while the other four are Army Chaplains. Two lieutenant colonels and two colonels were also in the pool of chaplains who participated in the pre-test. Of the Army captains none were first term chaplains. A first term chaplain is one who is fulfilling their initial three years of service in the chaplaincy. My intent by administering the pre-test questionnaire was to validate my assumption that chaplains have experienced burnout, to identify some causes of burnout, to understand how chaplains personally conduct self-care, to validate that the Chaplain Corps has no intentional self-care model, to identify that there is a great need to place an emphasis on self-care in the form of a model, to ensure that the questions made sense and to make appropriate corrections. The overall results from the pretest questionnaires showed that there is a need for a model of self-care in the Chaplain Corps. The pre-test questionnaires led me to simplify some of the questions and to include more personal information in the questionnaire. The personal information added was number of deployments, the marital status, denominational affiliation, number of children, number of CPE units, and ethnic background. The final and approved questionnaire can be located in (Appendix B: Questionnaire).

Previous and Current Chaplain Corps Self-Care Guidelines and Promotion

There have been attempts to foster self-care and deepen ministry. The Covenant and Code of Ethics for Chaplains of the Armed Forces reads with respect to self-care:

> I will maintain a disciplined ministry in such ways as keeping hours of prayer
> and devotion, endeavoring to maintain wholesome family relationships and

regularly engaging in educational and recreational activities for professional and personal development. I will seek to maintain good health habits.[79]

The Covenant and Code of Ethics offers guidelines for self-care when it speaks directly to spiritual disciplines (prayer and devotion), family (relational), educational development (mental), recreation (physical), and good health habits. Several good self-care strategies have been identified.

In 2000, the 20th Chief of Chaplains developed a strategic plan to develop a deeper spiritual life in the Unit Ministry Team. Under "Spiritual Leadership Goals and Objectives" 1.1.1, 1.1.2, and 1.1.7 the mandate is clear:

> Initiate a program to train total chaplaincy on how to give and receive spiritual direction by 4th quarter FY 2001. Initiate program to include a spiritual development plan in every chaplain's Officer Evaluation Report (OER) Support Form 67-9-1 by 4th quarter FY 2001...Conduct spiritual development workshops and retreats at each installation for Unit Ministry Team and family members by 4th quarter FY 2001.[80]

The 22nd Chief of Chaplains has enhanced the Chaplain Corps Strategic Campaign Plan, 2008-2013 to fulfill its collective calling to meet the religious and spiritual needs of America's Army. The Chaplain Corps Strategic Campaign Plan is nested with the four strategic goals of the Army Campaign Plan. The four strategic goals of the Army Campaign plan are:

> *Army Goal 1*: Provide Relevant and Ready Land Power
> *Army Goal 2*: Train and Equip Soldiers and Grow Adaptive Leaders
> *Army Goal 3*: Sustain an All-Volunteer Force
> *Army Goal 4*: Provide Infrastructure and Support

Under the Army Goal 4: Provide Infrastructure and Support, the Chaplaincy is supporting and advising Commanders in providing the platform for the free exercise of religion. The best way for the Chaplaincy to accomplish these objectives is to strengthen the spiritual life of the U.S. Army Chaplaincy. In order to be successful, the individual chaplains need to be spiritually strong. One way to accomplish this is to:

> Include a spiritual development plan in every Chaplain Officer Evaluation Report (OER) Support Form 67-9-1b. Conduct annual spiritual development

---

[79] A project of the National Conference on Ministry to the Armed Forces (NCMAF), February 2003.
[80] U.S. Army Chief of Chaplains, The U.S. Army Chaplaincy Strategic Plan FY 2000-2005, (Washington, D.C.: Government Printing Office, August, 2000), 11.

workshops or retreats at institutional level and above for UMT and family members.[81]

Other ways the Chaplain Corps promotes self-care is through mentoring training, reintegration training, and spiritual leadership conferences; this is a non-exhaustive list. Chaplain (COL) Richard Hartsell has written a dissertation entitled, Developing a Mentoring Training Program for Unit Ministry Teams at Fort Benning, Georgia: Preparation for Servant Leadership in the Twenty-First Century Army." From his dissertation he developed a UMT mentoring training program with training syllabus. Chaplain Hartsell's UMT mentoring training program has been a baseline for mentor training across the U.S. Army Chaplaincy.

The focus groups at WRAMC and Oblate School of Theology assisted in leading me to use a questionnaire process. The questionnaire developed by first conducting a per-version. The pre-test was enhanced based upon comments from the two cohort groups. The final questionnaire was administered to twenty-nine chaplains. Twenty-six questionnaires were collected and the information consolidated pointing to the majority of chaplains experiencing burnout and their need for a self-care model. The data collected from the questionnaires proves my hypothesis that "there is a need of a formal and/or informal model of self-care in the United States Army Chaplaincy."

---

[81] U.S. Army Chief of Chaplains, The U.S. Army Chaplaincy Strategic Plan FY 2008-2013, (Washington, D.C.: Government Printing Office, March, 2007).

CHAPTER FIVE

CRITICAL RESULTS OF THE PASTORAL RESEARCH

Introduction

In the "Questionnaire Data" section are the transcriptions of the chaplain applicants' actual replies to the questions presented in the questionnaires. Their entire answers were recorded so as not to bias the data collection. Their answers have not been edited or changed in any form unless noted for clarification purposes. I did not include any names, especially those chaplain applicants I sought clarification from with their written answers and the two chaplains I interviewed. I officially handed out twenty-nine questionnaires, but collected twenty-six questionnaires during the period of 2003 to 2005.

The data shows and proves my hypothesis that "there is a need of a formal and/or informal model of self-care in the United States Army Chaplaincy." The Chaplain Corps can and must put more attention in this area!

It seems to me that one chaplain applicant, number twenty six, stands out from the rest. The other participants appeared to be very willing to participate. When given the questionnaire, chaplain applicant twenty-six took the questionnaire to complete it, but returned it blank without any explanation.

Note – Each chaplain applicant had been given a number. All questions asked are listed with their replies. The questionnaires were distributed by myself in person or via electronic mail. Once I collected the questionnaires, I called, met with them in person or corresponded by email to clarify the chaplain applicant's replies if needed.

The results of the questionnaire are: thirteen out of twenty-six chaplains had heard of the Covenant and Code of Ethics for Chaplains of the Armed Forces and seven out of twenty-six chaplains had not, fourteen out of twenty-six chaplains had experienced burnout and six had not experienced burnout. Some of the reasons contributing to burnout were echoed among those completing the questionnaire: precious time spent away from family (missing births, birthdays and anniversaries), dogmatic workload, long duty hours, high operations tempo (time spent away from home station executing field training exercises, temporary duty assignment, peacekeeping missions and / or combat missions), little resources, little to no time for self-care, unrealistic expectations from superiors, and being overworked. Six out of twenty chaplains knew of someone in ministry that experienced burnout. Nine chaplains had a spiritual mentor or director and seven did not. Four chaplains mentioned that they sought counsel from a friend.

Fourteen out of twenty-six chaplains' ecclesiastical denomination promoted some formal or informal model of self-care requirements and procedures. Of the fourteen, some chaplains carried with them wisdom from senior or more mature ministers. Eleven out of twenty-six chaplains, upon entering the chaplaincy, had no formal or informal self-care requirements and procedures. Nineteen of the twenty-six chaplains had one or more units of Clinical Pastoral Education.

Deployment status consists of the chaplains interviewed: sixteen out of twenty-six deployed once, three out of twenty-six deployed twice, and seven out of the twenty-six never deployed.

There were eighteen ecclesiastical denominations represented: Assemblies of God (3), Southern Baptist Church (3), Free Will Baptist (2), United Methodist Church (3), Nondenominational (2), Progressive Baptist (2), National Baptist Convention USA, Inc. (1), Lutheran Church - Missouri Synod (1), Presbyterian Church of America (1), Roman Catholic (1), Church of the Latter Day Saints (1), United Pentecostal (1), Evangelical Free Church of America (1), Bible Fellowship Church (1), Church of God (1), Chaplaincy Full Gospel Churches (1), and American Baptist (1). The American Baptist chaplain applicant was the one that turned in a blank questionnaire form.

Questionnaire Data Collection

Question #1: State your self-care techniques. Self-care can be defined as the acknowledgement of who one is spiritually, mentally, and physically and the care needed to maintain effective job performance and holistic wellness.

Chaplain Applicant #1-Time for reflection, enjoy the beauty of creation i.e. take trips to different states each year.

Chaplain Applicant #2-Have a couple close friends.

Chaplain Applicant #3-Perform daily devotions, attend worship services that I'm not conducting, exercise regularly and do crossword puzzles.

Chaplain Applicant #4-I find that spending time in the woods, surrounded by nature works, refreshes me the most. Comedy (Slap Stick) always lightens my mood. Soft music while suffering the Internet w/o distractions helps calm me down.

Chaplain Applicant #5-I am INTJ, and recognize that I can become overwhelmed with people, particularly with crisis counseling. I am careful to protect my "cave time." That is time where I can disengage and participate in an activity that I enjoy. I have many hobbies, which play a key role in my self-care. At home I am working on a model railroad, I paint miniatures and I am engaged in a couple academic research projects. Many of my hobbies are intense and require concentration. For the most part, I don't mind maintaining a level of intensity. For me self-care involves periodically disengaging from ministry and finding something I enjoy engaging in. While deployed I painted military miniatures on my off time. This provided me small breaks from ministry, in which I could restore myself.

Chaplain Applicant #6-Daily office conversations with wife and spiritual directors, church attendance, communion, reading.

Chaplain Applicant #7-Pray, exercise, read humorous books, plan time with wife, and laugh through absurdities.

Chaplain Applicant #8-Exercise, reading, television, and talking it out with close friends and confidants.

Chaplain Applicant #9-Exercise, music, diet, journaling, time alone to sit and think. Key: viewing self-care as body and soul or physical and spiritual.

Chaplain Applicant #10-My self-care technique includes proper rest, diet, exercise, meditation, vacation at the beach and mountains, listening to soothing and relaxing music. Getting away from the hustle and bustle of life and retreat with the Lord and sacred writing like Scripture, good devotions such as 'My Utmost for His Highest' and 'Streams in the Desert.' Journaling has been extremely effective tools for self-care.

Chaplain Applicant #11-Morning devotions, prayers during the day and talking to mentor during the week.

Chaplain Applicant #12-Leave the work place in time to eat dinner at home with family, regular talks/meetings with chaplain buddies and exercise plus play.

Chaplain Applicant #13-Home yard work, hunting/fishing and periodic debriefing sessions with a select group of men.

Chaplain Applicant #14-

1. Do work in hour blocks then reward myself to do something I want to do-whether it is with myself or with family.
2. Spend time gardening or landscaping.

Chaplain Applicant #15-swimming, meditation and needle point.

Chaplain Applicant #16- video graphics and walking.

Chaplain Applicant #17-Bible study, family time, music, and devotions.

Chaplain Applicant #18-

Physical: proper nutrition, rest, and exercise.
Spiritual: personal devotions (Scripture and prayer), family devotions, corporate worship, and practice of spiritual disciplines.

Chaplain Applicant #19-Sleep/naps, physical exercise, reading and playing guitar.

Chaplain Applicant #20-Daily bible reading, daily prayer, daily starbucks and four days a week gym.

Chaplain Applicant #21-Vacations with family-must be intentional, active in daily spiritual devotions, active in worship, active in accountability group- @ Fort Sill with three chaplains-I am currently seeking a group now.

Chaplain Applicant #22-Devotional life and prayer, T.V.-sports and news, P.T. and time with wife-going out/movie/weekend-very few!

Chaplain Applicant #23-Eating well, tasking naps, vacations (short weekends) and exercise.

Chaplain Applicant #24-

1. Daily devotional, personal/family i.e. scriptures and prayer.
2. Regular church attendance and activities-off post normally.
3. Take time for family and spouse just having fun.

Chaplain Applicant #25-I lay down for a short 15-20 minutes of rest and reflection, prayer and personal spiritual reflection/Bible reading and playing with my children.

Chaplain #Applicant #26-Did not complete question.

Brief Analysis: Overwhelmingly the chaplains used prayer, scripture readings, attending and participating in church services/ activities when some else is conducting the worship services/events, rest, proper diet, exercise, spending time with family, laughter, outdoor activities, journaling and pausing between the hustle and bustle of life.

Question #2: What is the Chaplain's Corp history of self-care? (i.e. formal or informal)

Chaplain Applicant #1-Not good! We tend to be work-a-holics. We have the savior complex.

Chaplain Applicant #2-Limited, if at all.

Chaplain Applicant #3-For Priest they have an annual retreat and monthly days of reflection. Protestants and others develop their own informal techniques.

Chaplain Applicant #4-Very informal! I have spoken to the Installation's Family Life Chaplain several times concerning the need of 'Caring for the Caregiver.' He's aware as well as several other key leaders within the Chaplaincy, yet what has really been done?

Chaplain Applicant #5-Spotty at best. The official policy of the Chaplain's Corps seems to me a set of mixed messages. We say that it's important to care for our families and ourselves. But then we expect chaplains to prepare Soldiers/families for deployment, deploy and reintegrate Soldiers and families, without recognizing the needs of that UMT. Informal mentorship by Command Chaplains has been far more fruitful for me. I have had several Command Chaplains who have encouraged me to be proactive in my self-care. I've also had mentors who plainly addressed issues related to spiritual renewal and healing. One reminder that has remained with me came from a chaplain friend of mine. "Remember that spiritual restoration takes longer than physical or mental restoration. When you pour yourself into people, it takes more time to renew than it does other officers to recover from a rigorous STAFFEX."

> NOTE-STAFFEX stands for staff exercise. The intent behind a STAFFEX is to build a working relationship among the staff while working on several projects under a time restraint.

Chaplain Applicant #6-I think chaplains have always been able to connect with other chaplains to receive care. I'm not sure of the complete history.

Chaplain Applicant #7-Informal, occasional discussion and training on the subject.

Chaplain Applicant #8-Exercise for stress management, counseling with pastors, and leave and retreats.

Chaplain Applicant #9-Formal promotion of spiritual care. Very little practical "How To" done on the local line beyond going home on time.

Chaplain Applicant #10-Biannual retreats for junior leaders and senior leaders. Protestant and Priest have self-care conference where they can get away and recharge their emotional and spiritual batteries. We also meet in each others homes and places of worship for self-care. We spend time thinking and reflecting on how we can take good care of ourselves.

Chaplain Applicant #11-Encouragement in "practicing what one preaches" concerning empowerment for living from the same message one is preaching.

Chaplain Applicant #12-I don't know.

Chaplain Applicant #13-Sporadic division or installation-wide annual UMT retreats. Monthly UMT Training events that too-briefly mention "self-care." Occasionally supervisory chaplains schedule UMT Training days away from the office. For the most part, the Corps talks a self-care game, but doesn't intentionally, routinely require it of their subordinates.

Chaplain Applicant #14-I am not sure?

Chaplain Applicant #15-It has been a mixed bag from great support to Chaplains that don't believe in compensation time or days off. Often times, commanders have been more supportive than chaplains.

Chaplain Applicant #16-Not to well.

Chaplain Applicant #17-?

Chaplain Applicant #18-USAF Chaplain Service encourages Chaplains to tend to the garden of their souls through personal and corporate worship. Moreover, the USAF Chaplains are authorized 15 days each year for denominational conferences, spiritual retreats, etc…

Chaplain Applicant #19-None know.

Chaplain Applicant #20-Too busy and not leading by example. Lacking in devotions and P.T.

Chaplain Applicant #21-Depends on installation, BDE, etc. Possibly a day retreat.

Chaplain Applicant #22-Poor, None issued and Don't know: never heard of it.

Chaplain Applicant #23-Formal: retreats Informal: None that I know of.

Chaplain Applicant #24-

1. Korea= 2 times per year-Ministry in Korea Workshop.
2. Fort Hood=Once in 3 years and 1 day offsite spiritual retreat called "Pastor Burnout" actually led by hospital chaplain.

Informal-Slipping out when need arises-good time management.

Chaplain Applicant #25-I know we must have a plan listed on our OER support form. There is a lot of freedom to do whatever we want, since the Corps is so diverse.

Chaplain Applicant #26- Did not complete question.

Brief Analysis: The majority of chaplain applicants knew of no formal Chaplain Corps history of self-care. The applicants spoke of mixed messages by the Corps. For example, encouraging chaplains to conduct self-care, but not practicing it. Some chaplains had positive experiences of retreats (#24). For the most part there was nothing formal, but there was a need to receive some training in the area of self-care (#7 and #9).

Question #3 Have you experienced burnout? Burnout is defined as a temporary disability that prevents one from effective job performance.

Chaplain Applicant #1-No! I work long hours if necessary. I also take time for self-maintenance during down time. This has been the key to my success through the years.

Chaplain Applicant #2-No.

Chaplain Applicant #3-Yes.

Chaplain Applicant #4-Yes.

Chaplain Applicant #5-Yes, but not as a long-term condition.

Chaplain Applicant #6-Somewhat, but not quite yet in the Chaplaincy.

Chaplain Applicant #7-Yes.

Chaplain Applicant #8-Yes.

Chaplain Applicant #9-No, but I believe I have been close. I call it "brown out."

Chaplain Applicant #10-No, I have not experienced burnout, however, I begin to wonder sometimes when my job performance as a major was not peaking consistently as it did as a captain. I soon realize that my ratings were not what I expected because I could not keep a job for more than a year at a time. The six years I served as a major I had five different assignments. No burnout, but questioned my performance rating for a while. The Lord blessed me in spite of the limited thinking at the time.

Chaplain Applicant #11-No.

Chaplain Applicant #12-Yes.

Chaplain Applicant #13-Twice, as a battalion chaplain. As a supervisory chaplain, when I see it building, I just clear the schedule and go home. 12-24 extra hours are usually adequate to get through the log jam.

Chaplain Applicant #14-At times.

Chaplain Applicant #15-Yes, to a degree, more being overwhelmed by too much to do and too many expectations that were unrealistic-constant 'do more with less syndrome.'

Chaplain Applicant #16- No.

Chaplain Applicant #17-Yes. Post seminary, pastoring Seventh Day Adventist with some mean spirited congregation members. <u>I was driven and unbalanced.</u>

Chaplain Applicant #18-No-God is good-All the time-Can I get a witness?

Chaplain Applicant #19-Yes.

Chaplain Applicant #20-Yes.

Chaplain Applicant #21-No.

Chaplain Applicant #22-Yes.

Chaplain Applicant #23-Yes!

Chaplain Applicant #24-Yes.

Chaplain Applicant #25-Yes!

Chaplain Applicant #26- Did not complete question.

<u>Brief Analysis:</u> Chaplain applicant number three spoke about experiencing burnout prior to entering the chaplaincy. Perhaps, in civilian ministry? Correction to question-should have asked 'did you experience burnout in civilian ministry or as a chaplain?' Out of the twenty-five chaplain applicants that answered the question seventeen answered 'yes' to experiencing burnout and eight answered 'no' to experiencing burnout. Of the chaplains that experienced burnout it appeared they developed or enhanced their self-care techniques on the spot to assist in eliminating the symptoms.

Question #3a: If so, why?

Chaplain Applicant #1-N/A.

Chaplain Applicant #2-N/A.

Chaplain Applicant #3-Due to a failure to follow proper self-care and to seek outside help when overwhelmed.

Chaplain Applicant #4-I became overwhelmed with things that I/Command felt needed to be done, and I started feeling anxious, less concentrated. I'd say typical "Stressed" symptoms; once these symptoms became more induced my sleep pattern got out of whack, which then intensified the already stressed period.

Chaplain Applicant #5-There are times that the mission requires more of us than we have to give. I believe that the saying goes, "God never gives more than we can handle" is a lie. I cannot imagine anyone really "handling" the death of a spouse or child. I do believe that His grace is sufficient, and abundant. However, that does not mean that at points I may become overwhelmed. The peace I find rests in the reality that God is right there with me. And, as the Master of time and space, knows where He plans to carry me.

Chaplain Applicant #6-The competing demands of family and my own ideas about how much I should be at work.

Chaplain Applicant #7-When I don't pray and play, I burnout. It's that simple.

Chaplain Applicant #8-Due to overwork and commitments. Too much mission and little resources.

Chaplain Applicant #9-This happen because I did not practice any self renewing rituals. I did not exercise, journal, rest properly, pray at a depth that was renewing for me or read scripture beyond sermon preparation.

Chaplain Applicant #10-N/A.

Chaplain Applicant #11-N/A.

Chaplain Applicant #12-In my own diagnosis, to some, short-lived, superficial extent…I've felt overwhelmed with multiple tasks with deadlines upon which career advancement lingered.

Chaplain Applicant #13-My lack of self-awareness to the stresses of unit OPTEMPO.

Chaplain Applicant #14- Trying to achieve what I perceived to be expectations from my supervisors.

Chaplain Applicant #15-More with less syndrome, unrealistic expectations and lack of superior's support.

Chaplain Applicant #16-N/A.

Chaplain Applicant #17-Driven to perform without taking into account my need to be balanced.

Chaplain Applicant #18-N/A.

Chaplain Applicant #19-Too many responsibilities.

Chaplain Applicant #20-My first active duty assignment, I was coming to work from 0600-1900. I was there for a little over a year and not taking care of myself spiritually at a Basic Training BN. Never again!

> NOTE-0600-1900 is based on the twenty-four hour time clock. The twelve hour time clock equals to 6:00 a.m. to 7:00 p.m.

Chaplain Applicant #21- I have been tired from limited leave returning from deployment (lost leave) and hurried PCS.

Chaplain Applicant #22- In Iraq-waiting to come home. A few other chaplains and civilian pastors. The chaplains due to deployment and the civilian pastors due to being overworked.

Chaplain Applicant #23-I was not allowed (by military standards) to grieve or show emotional weakness. By military standards officers are not allowed to show weakness for any reason!

Chaplain Applicant #24- Korea 8-9 months in the tour.

Chaplain Applicant #25- No time off and long hours. While deployed to Kosovo I worked 7 days a week/18 hour days. That's with no time off. Also, from my own unhealthy motivations of "being-vs.-doing." Low self esteem and strong passion and sense of calling. Also, a lack of close supervision by another chaplain to say "slow down!"

Chaplain Applicant #26- Did not complete question.

Brief Analysis:

Some intra-personal factors were listed as: Failure to seek help within or out of the military, sense of calling, overfunctioning, self-neglect, managing stress and lost of leave.

Several inter-personal factors listed were: unrealistic expectations from supervisors, poor supervision from staff command and technical chain of commands, OPTEMPO, lack of resources-do more with less, and long hours.

Loosing annual leave days is a systemic problem in the military and Soldiers of all ranks fit into this category. Many times the chaplain feels the need not to take leave because the needs of the military are greater. When the chaplain does take leave many times it is a working leave. Working leave means the chaplain is on leave status, but continuing to work. The chaplain and other Soldiers take working leave because loosing leave reflects negatively on the chain of command. The implied concern is that the command is not caring for their Soldiers by allowing them to take leave. Another example of being on leave status, but not enjoying their leave is due to preparing for a permanent change of station (PCS) move. A PCS move by nature is very exhausting. Some of the PCS responsibilities for the Soldiers are to clear each installation and handle personal concerns. Very seldom is PCS leave used to relax. It is intermingled with work!

Question #4: Do you know of anyone who has experienced burnout?

Chaplain Applicant #1-Yes.

Chaplain Applicant #2-N/A.

Chaplain Applicant #3-Yes.

Chaplain Applicant #4-Yes.

Chaplain Applicant #5-Yes.

Chaplain Applicant #6-Yes.

Chaplain Applicant #7-Yes.

Chaplain Applicant #8-Yes.

Chaplain Applicant #9-Yes.

Chaplain Applicant #10-Yes.

Chaplain Applicant #11-Yes.

Chaplain Applicant #12-Not sure…

Chaplain Applicant #13-Yes.

Chaplain Applicant #14-Yes.

Chaplain Applicant #15-Yes.

Chaplain Applicant #16-Yes.

Chaplain Applicant #17-Yes.

Chaplain Applicant #18-No, not personally. I've only heard of individuals who have experienced "burnout," but I have no personal knowledge of their circumstances or situations.

Chaplain Applicant #19-Yes.

Chaplain Applicant #20-Not first hand, but I could say I have observed it.

Chaplain Applicant #21-Yes.

Chaplain Applicant #22-Yes, a few other chaplains and pastors.

Chaplain Applicant #23-Yes.

Chaplain Applicant #24- Most chaplains felt the same way.

Chaplain Applicant #25-Yes.

Chaplain Applicant #26- Did not complete question.

<u>Brief Analysis:</u>
The overwhelming reply to question four is 'yes.'

Question #4a: If so, what were the causes?

Chaplain Applicant #1-Many of my fellow chaplains burned out simply because they took no time out for themselves or family.

Chaplain Applicant #2-N/A.

Chaplain Applicant #3-

1. Too much work and no play (relaxation).
2. A failure to maintain proper spiritual focus.
3. Too much stress and not enough rewards.

Chaplain Applicant #4-Too great of a work load brought on about by poor time management; I'd even add poor assessment of Soldier's needs. Example: If one continues responding to what Soldiers deem as emergencies without properly assessing the validity of these emergencies we'd constantly be engrossed and overworked.

Chaplain Applicant #5-For some, it's failure to balance the needs of the moment (25m targets) with the long term needs (2000m targets) of our families and ourselves. These are times we need to surge and put in the hours. Far too many officers and NCOs live in the work of "glass balls," fearful that letting anything drop will result in a loss of their own identity and/or personhood. I think much of the problem is rooted in the identity we choose to claim for ourselves.

Chaplain Applicant #6-The person I am thinking of was unprepared emotionally and mentally for ministry and was trying to exorcise his own demons by ministering in difficult places.

Chaplain Applicant #7-OPTEMPO and not having a mentor.

Chaplain Applicant #8-Too much mission and little resources.

Chaplain Applicant #9-They worked too hard, did not delegate, had no one to talk too, etc.

Chaplain Applicant #10-Lack of self-care and lack of spiritual accountability. What I observe is that they chose not to take the time to process their disabilities or inadequacies in honest and real way. Seek help from a confidant and friend who will be there for you in the darkest night of the soul.

Chaplain Applicant #11-Their self-care was none existent or included more addictive behavior than productive habits. It did not usually occur during life crisis. Rather it occurred in the midst of a healthy personal concept of ministry.

Chaplain Applicant #12-Left blank.

Chaplain Applicant #13-OPTEMPO.

Chaplain Applicant #14- I think it can be partial Army fault and partial chaplain fault.

Chaplain Applicant #15-Family problems, more with less syndrome, unrealistic expectations and lack of superior's support.

Chaplain Applicant #16-Overworked.

Chaplain Applicant #17-Don't know, assume similar to mine.

Chaplain Applicant #18-N/A.

Chaplain Applicant #19-Bad personal boundaries and willingness to accept more work.

Chaplain Applicant #20-

1. Too many hours of work, 10-16 hours per day.
2. Not taking days off or leave.
3. Family friction.
4. Lack of daily devotions for eschatological energy.

Chaplain Applicant #21-Difficult commander wanted me to pick up extra duties outside my role as a chaplain, OPTEMPO, etc.

Chaplain Applicant #22-Deployment and overworked.

Chaplain Applicant #23-Not allowed to express themselves emotionally.

Chaplain Applicant #24- Too much counseling loads from depressed Soldiers, very late night and daily ministry.

Chaplain Applicant #25-Many of the same reasons as mine.

Chaplain Applicant #26- Did not complete question.

Brief Analysis:

Chaplain applicant number fourteen stated burnout is partially the chaplain's fault and Army's fault. There were some issues the chaplain needed to own up to. For example; being out of balance spiritually, sacrificing quality family time, and neglecting taking productive leave, failure to implement self-care techniques and not seeking outside assistance. Fault from the military side is due to being overworked, numerous deployments, family separations, long hours and high OPTEMPO.

Question #5: If you have experienced burnout, what type of help did you seek, if any?

Chaplain Applicant #1-N/A.

Chaplain Applicant #2-N/A.

Chaplain Applicant #3-

1. Pastoral Counseling
2. Medical assistance to aid in proper rest and sleep.
3. Reinstituted my self-care plan.

Chaplain Applicant #4-

First, I vented / down loaded / dumped on to another minister (I guess looking for sympathy).

Second, I then took a break, readjusted my priorities, reestablished / re-looked at my relationship with God, which was out of balance.

Finally, I also found that refocusing on my wife and children reminded me that these folks are my primary responsibility as directed by God, not the Army nor the Soldiers in it.

Chaplain Applicant #5-Self assessment.

Chaplain Applicant #6-I suppose I pray, fast, and try to relax and put my job in perspective against the larger struggles of the world.

Chaplain Applicant #7-I have sought out help with peers and mentors.

Chaplain Applicant #8-Took leave and exercised.

Chaplain Applicant #9-N/A.

Chaplain Applicant #10-Christian counseling has helped as well as Christian pastoral therapist.

Chaplain Applicant #11-N/A.

Chaplain Applicant #12-

1. Prayer.
2. Leave work and later readdress tasks to be completed.
3. Organize tasks and outline solutions.
4. Commiserate with chaplain buddies.
5. Get consolation and encouragement from wife.
6. Exercise.

Chaplain Applicant #13-Unit medics, TMC PA/Dr., trusted mental health folks.

Chaplain Applicant #14-I gutted it out. I did not seek any professional help.

Chaplain Applicant #15-Counseling and support from United Methodist pastors outside the military.

Chaplain Applicant #16-N/A.

Chaplain Applicant #17-Came in Air Force. Took much more time for self.

Chaplain Applicant #18-N/A.

Chaplain Applicant #19-Talk with a chaplain peer.

Chaplain Applicant #20-Exhausted from long hours of work without a break.

Chaplain Applicant #21-No.

Chaplain Applicant #22-None.

Chaplain Applicant #23- Counsel without informing the military.

Chaplain Applicant #24-Had pneumonia twice, so got quarters for a couple of days. Many chaplains get run down in Korea.

Chaplain Applicant #25-Yes. My depression shut me down to staring at my PC for 3 hours. I checked myself over at department of Behavior Medical. I'm now seeing a Military Family Therapist off post with my spouse. I'm being treated for "PTSD" and "AD HD" with counseling and medication, also CPE training.

Chaplain Applicant #26- Did not complete question.

Brief Analysis:

Chaplain applicant number fourteen sadly mentioned that he did not seek any professional help with his burnout, but gutted it out! Sadly enough, sometime this reply is the unwritten rule. Chaplain applicant number seventeen reply is devastating. I interviewed the chaplain, reference his reply, and the he stated, "The OPTEMPO was draining on his family and himself. He wanted and felt called to a different genre of military ministry." He was looking for a pastoral parish setting without the unneeded challenges of vying time with his family, unit and congregation that he was providing pastoral leadership to. He had experienced burnout and felt the symptoms would only get better by changing military services.

Question #5a: If assistance was sought, did you maintain or improve your self-care techniques?

Chaplain Applicant #1-N/A.

Chaplain Applicant #2-N/A.

Chaplain Applicant #3-Yes.

Chaplain Applicant #4-No. The assistance I sought was temporary. I'm hard-headed, self-care techniques work, and I promote them; however, I must come to that place or the rationalization that I'm burning out before I implement a plan. Until I'm ready and say enough is enough a plan / program doesn't work well for me. I'm even a procrastinator when it comes to self-care.

Chaplain Applicant #5-Yes. I completed what needed to be done, and disengaged as soon as practical. In the past my challenge has been: One, recognizing that I was too engaged, or Two, being willing to disengage when I was no longer required. I have to work to build my own awareness of my level of engagement and honestly assessing if my level of engagement is appropriate for the circumstances and calling of God for that moment. These challenges still get me, but I'm growing.

Chaplain Applicant #6-Yes, assistance always helps my self-care.

Chaplain Applicant #7-Improved.

Chaplain Applicant #8-N/A.

Chaplain Applicant #9-N/A.

Chaplain Applicant #10-When an individual seeks assistance that means to me that they want to improve their self-care techniques.

Chaplain Applicant #11-N/A.

Chaplain Applicant #12-Maintain; I've yet to add a distressing hobby.

Chaplain Applicant #13-Maintain.

Chaplain Applicant #14-N/A.

Chaplain Applicant #15-Yes, maintained-kept support channels open.

Chaplain Applicant #16-N/A.

Chaplain Applicant #17-Improved.

Chaplain Applicant #18-N/A.

Chaplain Applicant #19-Yes, gave me perspective to correct.

Chaplain Applicant #20-No assistance sought. I changed myself by ensuring spirited fitness before or at work through the Word and Prayer.

Chaplain Applicant #21-N/A.

Chaplain Applicant #22-None.

Chaplain Applicant #23-Improved.

Chaplain Applicant #24- After ministry in Korea chaplains did feel much better.

Chaplain Applicant #25-Greatly improved.

Chaplain Applicant #26- Did not complete question.

Brief Analysis:
If assistance was sought by agencies inside or outside the military the chaplain greatly benefited.

Question #6: In your opinion, evaluate the Chaplain Corps emphasis on self-care?

Chaplain Applicant #1-The chaplaincy is beginning to emphasize the need for time to care for our spiritual life.

Chaplain Applicant #2-Probably sincere; however, very difficult. There is no relevant program or opportunity.

Chaplain Applicant #3-There isn't a great focus on caring for one self. Our emphasis until recently has been on caring for others. Chaplains and chaplain assistants are our last focus.

Chaplain Applicant #4-They talk it up, yet aren't much to implement a plan / program. Look at Fort Hood, what has the Installation / Garrison done to promote self-care. Oh, we had one event in Belton (Catholic Retreat Center). The chaplaincy is under manned and the workload is ever increasing, so there isn't time for self-care. The mission must be accomplished.

Chaplain Applicant #5-I don't think the Chaplain Corps has a clue how to do this. We all recognize the need, but our context does not reinforce success. In fact the context may reinforce failure. I was recently asked, after attending 8 notional deaths during a hospital exercise, what do I do to take care of myself? The question reinforced the reality that Chaplains are often spread throughout the battlefield. Moreover, we are often not inclined to be vulnerable with each other (perhaps a hold-over from the competitive nature of civilian ministry). We are expected to carry heavy loads and often with little or no real retuned support.

Chaplain Applicant #6-Very high. I have had numerous chaplains encourage me to take care of myself. I think we do a good job of encouraging our colleagues, at least at my level. I can't speak for more senior chaplains.

Chaplain Applicant #7-It is encouraging, but we need to encourage the mentoring process. The one on one relationship is more important than just some TSP or conference, etc.

    NOTE-TSP stands for training support plan. It is a schedule to show how a particular unit will support certain training activities.

Chaplain Applicant #8-We talk a good game, but much is left up to each individual.

Chaplain Applicant #9-We talk a good game. After some good people have gotten into trouble we have put a mentoring plan into place that might have an indirect impact on possible burnout.

Chaplain Applicant #10-I rate the Chaplain Corps emphasis on self-care on a scale of 8 with 10 being the highest. One specific way this is done through the assignment process. Chaplain Career managers work with the individual chaplain and their future assignments to assist them with self-care. If a chaplain has had a couple tough assignments, then the chaplain branch tries to work out an assignment where the chaplain can get some relief and recharge his or her battery before they go back into the hard charging units.

Chaplain Applicant #11-It is hit or miss…it all depends on the supervisory climate. The formal encouragement is well articulated, but the expectation to be busy too often gets in the way.

Chaplain Applicant #12-Poor.

Chaplain Applicant #13-Does a significantly better job than the chain of command, but could still be more deliberate.

Chaplain Applicant #14-Non-existence.

Chaplain Applicant #15-Except for a few chaplains, it is non-existent. Self-care does not get rewarded. We don't practice what we preach.

Chaplain Applicant #16-Weak.

Chaplain Applicant #17-Good.

Chaplain Applicant #18-It's interesting the Air Force gives its chaplains 15 days while the United States Army gives 10 days. It would be interesting to find out how many the United States Navy gives chaplains.

Chaplain Applicant #19-Non-existent.

Chaplain Applicant #20- Emphasis is external-helping others! But not internal-helping each other and ourselves.

Chaplain Applicant #21-Limited. Do not really know of an overall program.

Chaplain Applicant #22-Poor.

Chaplain Applicant #23-Poor.

Chaplain Applicant #24-Need much more. Scale 1-10=2.

Chaplain Applicant #25-Still very little, until someone bites the dust and falls…

Chaplain Applicant #26- Did not complete question.

Brief Analysis:
Overall, the replies were that the Chaplain Corps has identified the need for wellness and is making efforts to improve the focus. Chaplain applicant number ten mentions the assignment branch takes under consideration the self-care needs of the chaplain as they manage his or her future assignments.

Question #7: In your experience what does burnout look like or identify some indicators of burnout?

Chaplain Applicant #1- Attitude, poor self image, little interest in one's job, family, spiritual life.

Chaplain Applicant #2-Burnout itself is an implosion of the individual. I watch for actions leading an individual to implode.

Chaplain Applicant #3-

1. A lack of desire to do ministry.
2. A depress feeling.
3. Lack of energy and motivation.

Chaplain Applicant #4-Feeling overwhelmed, lack of concentration, frustration, counter productivity, continually exhausted, edginess, emotional, isolated, basically anything that appears to be out of character for that individual.

Chaplain Applicant #5-I become very impatient and overly critical. I also tend to withdraw more readily.

Chaplain Applicant #6-The inability to stay in your current position because of stress. Sexual impotence. Severely strained relationships with just about everyone. Difficulty getting out of bed at 0530 in the morning.

Chaplain Applicant #7-Lose joy and passion for ministry, loss of sleep, irritability and mild depression.

Chaplain Applicant #8-Depression, anger/lashing out, poor work productivity and aloof.

Chaplain Applicant #9-Poor judgment, physical and mental fatigue.

Chaplain Applicant #10-Individual may be discouraged, depressed, disillusioned, sense of hopelessness and lack of purpose, meaning and satisfaction in like or job performance.

Chaplain Applicant #11-Mild burnout involves lack of motivation and a diminished joy in the ministry. Advanced burnout manifests itself in withdrawal / agitation and a lack of purpose as a minister.

Chaplain Applicant #12-Anger, isolation, apathy, sarcasm and illness.

Chaplain Applicant #13-Impatient, short tempered, tunnel vision, unable to look at big picture.

Chaplain Applicant #14-Mentally, spiritually, and physically fatigued. Worn out! Normally results in an apathetic and cynical behavior.

Chaplain Applicant #15-Hating your job, not wanting to go to work, no emotional barriers left and short fuse.

Chaplain Applicant #16-Don't want to deal with clients, tired, impatient and despair of being helpful.

Chaplain Applicant #17-Moody and insecure.

Chaplain Applicant #18-Fatigue-feeling drained, loss of passion for ministry and lack of motivation.

Chaplain Applicant #19-No days off, Need to carry cell phone/pager everywhere and no planned vacations.

Chaplain Applicant #20-Exhaustion, no time with family or friends, bed in office, no leave and lacking in spiritual fitness.

Chaplain Applicant #21-Unable to fully minister and Soldier.

Chaplain Applicant #22-Depression, bad attitude-not carrying and not wanting to minister.

Chaplain Applicant #23-Can't eat, can't sleep, or if I slept I was still tired. Can't concentrate, cranky and tearful.

Chaplain Applicant #24-Just feel tired, fried, maybe still does ministry, but very tired.

Chaplain Applicant #25-Ineffective ministry and poor family life.

Chaplain Applicant #26- Did not complete question.

Brief Analysis:
Burnout presents itself in physical, emotional, mental, and spiritual symptoms. The physical symptoms are changes in eating habits and weight, chronic fatigue, exhaustion, headaches, high blood pressure and increased susceptibility to illness. The emotional symptoms are anxiety, discouragement; feelings of failure, self-blame, self-pity and having nothing left to give; inability to enjoy leisure activities; loss of coping skills,

emotional control, self-esteem, self-confidence and humor; emotional exhaustion and social withdrawal. Mental symptoms are detachment, forgetfulness, rejection, loss of motivation, inability to reach decisions and to concentrate. Spiritual symptoms range from being angry with God, doubting one's call to ministry, lack of accountability, being unable to pray, questioning one's faith, and struggling with one's commitment to both God and ministry.

Question #8: Define self-care in your own language.

Chaplain Applicant #1- Self-care is time to do nothing, time to read, reflect on one's life's journey, quality time with God.

Chaplain Applicant #2-My ability to recognize my performance psyche such that I keep on a balanced whatever keel.

Chaplain Applicant #3-Self-care is doing those things which renew, strengthens and re-energizes you personally, spiritually and physically.

Chaplain Applicant #4- Being able to regulate one's physical, emotional and spiritual self in such a manner that they're always mindful of what's going on in their life, thus maintaining a balance.

Chaplain Applicant #5-Addressing my needs as a person. There is a difference between needs and wants. God says, that I should not "merely look out for my own personal interest, but also for the interests of others." Paul does not say that I should disregard either my needs or interests. My interests should be considered on the same level as the interests of others. I assume that I should do the same with my needs, though I recognize that an empty car won't run on platitudes. Sometimes, my need is mission essential. On the other hand I do think that it is implied that the need of another, should be considered above my wants (Rom. 13: 9-13 and Gal. 6:2-6). For me part of self-care is an awareness of the difference between need and want, and addressing my own needs as valid and valuable.

Chaplain Applicant #6-Maintaining my spiritual health through meaningful rituals.

Chaplain Applicant #7-

1. Spirituality-Going Deeper, not "smarter" in faith.
2. Maintaining good sleep and dietary habits.
3. Re-kindling joy of childhood.

Chaplain Applicant #8-Recreation and meditation (prayer).

Chaplain Applicant #9-A practice that keeps priorities (God, family and vocation) in order. It is renewing and sustaining because it (self-care) is based on spiritual principles.

Chaplain Applicant #10-Self-care is taking good care of self and being good to oneself with the full assurance that it is okay to treat oneself every now and then.

Chaplain Applicant #11-Applying the spiritual gifts that a minister sees so vital to the spiritual well-being of those to whom they minister to one's self.

Chaplain Applicant #12-Purposeful balance.

Chaplain Applicant #13-Ministering to or receiving ministry for…your own body, soul, and spirit.

Chaplain Applicant #14-Knowing my limits and knowing when to say enough is enough. Knowing how to say no!

Chaplain Applicant #15-Swimming daily, PT, meditating, sharing with spiritual director, time alone and music. "Calgon take me away!"

Chaplain Applicant #16-Anything that charges my batteries.

Chaplain Applicant #17-Taking time for balance.

Chaplain Applicant #18-Tending to the whole person, specifically spiritually and physically.

Chaplain Applicant #19-Separating oneself from one's work in such a way as to provide opportunities for physical relaxation, mental renewal, spiritual refreshment and family bonding.

Chaplain Applicant #20- Eight hour work day including PT (with exceptions), daily devotions, chill out at Starbucks daily and enjoying the God given pleasures of life.

Chaplain Applicant #21-Taking good care of self and family. Most be intentional in doing so.

Chaplain Applicant #22-Caring for my physical, spiritual, emotional needs and family needs in balance with ministry responsibilities.

Chaplain Applicant #23-Quiting when I am tired. Eating, resting and doing what I enjoy.

Chaplain Applicant #24-Being able to take a break, refresh, relax, be a brother for a while-And not a chaplain just for a second.

Chaplain Applicant #25-Making sure you are getting the right amount of food, rest and exercise. Also, having an accountability partner/chaplain. Also, a good mentor.

Chaplain Applicant #26- Did not complete question.

<u>Brief Analysis:</u>

Every chaplain applicant had some type of self-care strategy that addressed their spiritual (prayer), physical (exercise), emotional (time spent with family), and mental (reading) needs. One major change to their self-care strategies was finding balance.

Question #9: What civilian clergy self-care techniques (i.e. denominational) did you bring into the Chaplain Corp?

Chaplain Applicant #1- Meditation, time away from the office without feeling guilty.

Chaplain Applicant #2-None.

Chaplain Applicant #3-None.

Chaplain Applicant #4- Besides the theologically correct answers we learn in seminary, none. I was always taught in church that the harvest is plentiful and the laborers are few, so work hard and look forward to your rewards in heaven. The Southern Baptist Convention has recently begun beefing-up their Chaplaincy program, so I foresee many changes in how they begin relating to Chaplain needs, and more precisely their self-care venues.

Chaplain Applicant #5-My denomination is worse off than the Chaplain Corps. Church Planting ate my lunch because we were expected to "burn ourselves out for Jesus." Low pay, disrespect and exhaustion were supposed to be our badges of honor.

Chaplain Applicant #6-The wisdom of seeking council from senior pastors. A daily prayer life. Continuing education. Pastors from different denominations getting together. The importance of spending time with your wife.

Chaplain Applicant #7-None in particular. Learned what I needed to do while in the Army, through my own experiences.

Chaplain Applicant #8-None really…Well I guess prayer and meditation, but not necessarily from my denomination.

Chaplain Applicant #9-None: I did not take a day-off in the local parish and did not negotiate time off when I worked on Sunday in units I have served. NOT THE WAY TO OPERATE.

Chaplain Applicant #10-Prayer, Bible reading, reflection, journaling, relaxation techniques, and good old fashion R&R (Rest and Recuperation).

Chaplain Applicant #11-"Letting the word of Christ dwell in you richly…psalms and hymns and spiritual songs…making melody in your hearts to the Lord"

Chaplain Applicant #12-None.

Chaplain Applicant #13-I have great relations with my endorser and a couple of denominational minister friends in the Corps that I stay in touch with for self-care issues. My denomination also has a professional counseling center available to us Assemblies of God Chaplains at a 1-800-number.

Chaplain Applicant #14-Unfortunately, I did not bring any formal techniques.

Chaplain Applicant #15-My denominational (conference) requires that you be in a mentoring relationship with another United Methodist clergy. Back home they have groups that meet weekly within each district.

Chaplain Applicant #16-None-Bad out there too!

Chaplain Applicant #17-None.

Chaplain Applicant #18-Spiritual disciplines (prayer, worship, scripture, journaling, etc.), denominational conferences, retreats, spiritual renewal retreats and accountability Pastor groups.

Chaplain Applicant #19-

1. Days off are exactly <u>DAYS OFF</u>-if emergency, next day is the day off.
2. Recreational get-a-ways.

Chaplain Applicant #20- Weekly Bible Study, confession and Catechism Study.

Chaplain Applicant #21-The United Methodist Church encourages retreat time. My endorser has quarterly retreats-a time for rest and recharging one's batteries.

Chaplain Applicant #22-Used to play golf, but not since coming back in the Army-no time. Devotional life and family retreats.

Chaplain Applicant #23-None.

Chaplain Applicant #24-

1. Daily devotional, personal/family i.e. scriptures and prayer.
2. Regular church attendance and activities-off post normally.
3. Take time for family and spouse just having fun.

Chaplain Applicant #25-None. (SMILE)

Chaplain Applicant #26- Did not complete question.

Brief Analysis:

Many Chaplain applicants mentioned that their denomination offered little to no teaching on self-care. In fact, it was the opposite, burn yourself out for Jesus, you will reap your reward in heaven not on earth, rest is selfish, and burnout is a badge of courage. Sometime the chaplains were afraid to slow down in their ministry in fear of cheating God. The results from question eight, particularly chaplain applicant number sixteen, reinforces the need to teach self-care techniques.

Question #10: How do you conduct and how have you conducted self-care during garrison, FTX, peacekeeping operations, and combat deployments?

Chaplain Applicant #1-Left blank.

Chaplain Applicant #2-I go to lunch with my partner.

1. Chaplain Applicant #3- Sustain my spiritual devotion and life.
2. Exercise regularly.
3. Finding a spiritual buddy to share things with.

Chaplain Applicant #4- I workout and drink a lot of water. FTXs, and deployments are a nice change-of-pace. The focus becomes one "Ministering to Soldier." I don't have to fulfill all the other roles required of me. I also sleep better in the field with all the fresh air.

Chaplain Applicant #5-I painted most of an Acimenid Persian Army during an operational deployment.

Chaplain Applicant #6-By praying the in the office daily or wherever I find myself, FTX etcetera.

Chaplain Applicant #7-Devotionals, as much PT as possible, and laughing at absurdities.

Chaplain Applicant #8-Pryaer meetings, prayer partners, talking it out with a confidant and peer counsel.

Chaplain Applicant #9-

1. At My Best: Proper sleep, exercise, and spiritual nurture.
2. At My Worst: None of the above.

Chaplain Applicant #10-Steal away with myself and use imagination and imagery techniques to appropriate self-care without the luxury of time, place and space. Take mini-retreats in my spirit and soul. Take mental trips in my hooch / tent in Afghanistan. Dream dreams in the cold showers of Africa all the while thinking of the warmth of the creature comforts.

Chaplain Applicant #11-It seems to be the rule that the longer I was at a post or on a deployment the better I did with self-care. The initial excitement of the deployment would inevitably give way to the reality that if I was not taking care of myself, I would not be effective in taking care of others. Spiritual feeding and personal relax / recreation time would make all the difference in the world.

Chaplain Applicant #12-Generally talked about balance of spirit, mind and body!

Chaplain Applicant #13-I remind the staff formally of the needs through my daily chaplain devotionals, and informally as I circulate among the troops.

Chaplain Applicant #14-While deployed to Macedonia I would take time for myself to watch a movie, play pool, or other games.

Chaplain Applicant #15-Took the first hour of the day after 'stand to' as my time. I also met with Division Chaplain every couple of days for an hour.

Chaplain Applicant #16-Take a moment to read, reflect or run.

Chaplain Applicant #17-Always takes time to relate to family and get away at least one day a week.

Chaplain Applicant #18-Private devotional times, practice of the spiritual disciplines, proper nutrition, rest, personal hygiene, organized corporate worship opportunities (worship, Bible Studies) and fellowship opportunities.

Chaplain Applicant #19-

1. Field/Deployment-Minimum of one hour to myself with out interruptions.
2. Garrison-Planned/ intentional time-off.

Chaplain Applicant #20- Self-care-devotions daily everywhere.

Chaplain Applicant #21-Seeking God, exercise and back rubs from the wife.

Chaplain Applicant #22-I haven't.

Chaplain Applicant #23-When I am tired I quit!

Chaplain Applicant #24-I put on "Living a Balanced Life" for Soldiers for singles/ married, etc.

Chaplain Applicant #25-Time alone.

Chaplain Applicant #26- Did not complete question.

<u>Brief Analysis:</u>

Environments other than garrison settings require the chaplain to be innovative. Field training exercises and deployments offer different demands. The self-care techniques conducted in garrison will have to be altered. Field environments allow the chaplain to enjoy the beauty of nature God's creation. One thing that will never change is the chaplain being subject to "24/7" on-call duties. If on a rotating roster the chaplains has the opportunity to share on-call duties with other peers. On the other hand, if there is no one to share duties with the chaplain is subject to "24/7" on-call availability.

Question #11: Is there a need for a formal self-care module and/or program in the Chaplain Corps?

Chaplain Applicant #1- Absolutely!

Chaplain Applicant #2-A class at the career course. This is like morality, it cannot be delegated.

Chaplain Applicant #3-Yes.

Chaplain Applicant #4- Yes.

Chaplain Applicant #5-Can this kind of thing be taught in class? Perhaps the guidelines. Most of it needs to be fleshed out in relationships; particularly relationships with mentors.

Chaplain Applicant #6-I'm not sure. We already commit to some sort of daily prayer/ office in our chaplain corps covenant. I'm sure some formal training would be helpful to everyone.

Chaplain Applicant #7-Any attempt at a model may be helpful. Better than status quo. We all have more to learn in this area.

Chaplain Applicant #8-What you think CH Edison? You better believe there Is.

Chaplain Applicant #9-Yes, we see it all the time, but it becomes obvious when people break down or get into trouble.

Chaplain Applicant #10-I think that the formal self-care model is built into the scheduled retreats sponsored by the senior chaplains and Directorate of Ministry Initiatives.

Chaplain Applicant #11-Yes, but only as a suggested model. It would encourage / require chaplains to develop and use the model that best fits them and their faith.

Chaplain Applicant #12-Sure.

Chaplain Applicant #13-Yes. The Chaplain School could help by selecting only the very best chaplain instructors who are proven supervisory chaplains…mentoring, discipling, caring, etc.

Chaplain Applicant #14-I would vote for an informal module just because of my own resistance to forced Army programs.

Chaplain Applicant #15-Yes, in the fact that its necessity needs to be addressed. I will look different for each person.

Chaplain Applicant #16-Yes.

Chaplain Applicant #17-No, maybe?

Chaplain Applicant #18-Not necessarily "formal," for faith groups differ in their specific requirements. From a Christian perspective, one could offer an "informal" model of suggested practices.

Chaplain Applicant #19-Yes.

Chaplain Applicant #20-No! No government organized self-care module.

Chaplain Applicant #21-Yes!

Chaplain Applicant #22-Yes!

Chaplain Applicant #23-YES!

Chaplain Applicant #24-Yes.

Chaplain Applicant #25-Yes, also for how supervisor chaplains should monitor their chaplains.

Chaplain Applicant #26- Did not complete question.

Brief Analysis:
Overwhelmingly, the chaplain applicants have a desire for a self-care model. The desire is not to have a formal model, but an informal model and/or strategies. An informal model could be modified to fit each chaplain and their individual spiritual needs. An informal self-care model would provoke or invoke chaplains to conduct some form of wellness training.

Question #12: Are you and other Chaplains following the Covenant and Code of Ethics for Chaplains of the Armed Forces? It states: "I will maintain a disciplined ministry in such ways as keeping hours of prayer and devotion, endeavoring to maintain wholesome family relationships, and regularly engaging in educational and recreational activities for professional and personal development. I will seek to maintain good health habits."

Chaplain Applicant #1- I need you to explain this!

Chaplain Applicant #2-Mostly.

Chaplain Applicant #3-Yes.

Chaplain Applicant #4-No. The Covenant & Code of Ethic is a good model; however, when things begin to build-up and I'm expected to perform or accomplish the mission something will suffer and it is often me. The code becomes obsolete.

Chaplain Applicant #5-I assume that I am, though I'm not sure what that is.

Chaplain Applicant #6-Yes.

Chaplain Applicant #7-I have and continue to do my best in this area.

Chaplain Applicant #8-I strive for the ideal. But in reality this is the first I have heard of this code.

Chaplain Applicant #9-In a very lose way at times and at other times more so.

Chaplain Applicant #10-Yes.

Chaplain Applicant #11-Definitely…accountability and a personal sense of integrity go a long way in helping maintain a sensible and inspiring perspective on their ministry.

Chaplain Applicant #12-No; well, I'm not acquainted with it and I've never been "trained" on it.

Chaplain Applicant #13-Yes.

Chaplain Applicant #14-Yes. To a degree, but it could always stand improving.

Chaplain Applicant #15-I try, but don't always succeed.

Chaplain Applicant #16-No.

Chaplain Applicant #17-Yes, don't know.

Chaplain Applicant #18-Absolutely!

Chaplain Applicant #19-No-I feel it is flawed in some points and does not fully subscribe to their version of ethics.

Chaplain Applicant #20-Never saw it but-yes!

Chaplain Applicant #21-Yes, but during deployment, not possible.

Chaplain Applicant #22-First time hearing of the covenant.
I try, but often time not successful.

Chaplain Applicant #23-Yes. First time hearing of the covenant.

Chaplain Applicant #24-Yes of course.

Chaplain Applicant #25-This sounds good and I have a copy displayed on my office wall. I don't follow it very well. (SMILE)

Chaplain Applicant #26- Did not complete question.

Brief Analysis:
Surprising, several senior chaplains (COL) have not heard of the Covenant and Code of Ethics for Chaplains of the Armed Forces. Perhaps, training needs to be conducted periodically. Chaplain applicant number twelve commented about not being trained on the covenant and code of ethics.

Question #13: Do you have a spiritual director or mentor (military or civilian)? If so, how long have you had one? If not, why?

Chaplain Applicant #1- Yes.

Chaplain Applicant #2-Yes-several years.

Chaplain Applicant #3-No.

Chaplain Applicant #4-Yes. A military Chaplain for one year.

Chaplain Applicant #5-Yes, as suggested by Howard Hendrix, I try to keep a Paul, a Barnabas or two and a couple Timothy's in my life.

Chaplain Applicant #6-I have several with whom I often consult. The longest has been around for 6 years, others for less time.

Chaplain Applicant #7-I have a civilian mentor. My last assignment I had both military and civilian mentors. I am 5 months into this new job. I look for mentors constantly.

Chaplain Applicant #8-Beginning to establish one with local pastor. Less than a year.

Chaplain Applicant #9-I have not looked for one. My life might be better if I had one.

Chaplain Applicant #10-Yes, I have a couple mentors that have blessed me over thirty years.

Chaplain Applicant #11-Yes, retired Army Chaplains...one for three years... the most recent for one year.

Chaplain Applicant #12-No, but I have trustworthy friends (clergy) who as peers offer much pastor care.

Chaplain Applicant #13-Yes, and in addition, at each installation/Operation, I seek out an onsite mentor, a person of deep personal faith...sometimes a chaplain, sometimes not, sometimes senior to me, sometimes not.

Chaplain Applicant #14-I have a CPE Supervisor, consultant and therapist.

Chaplain Applicant #15-Yes, I have had one or the other the whole time I've been in the military. Some stations, I've had a mentor and others a spiritual director.

Chaplain Applicant #16-No.

Chaplain Applicant #17-No, not pursued.

Chaplain Applicant #18-Yes-since my answering the call to the Gospel ministry on 13 March 1988.

Chaplain Applicant #19-No.-No one I consider is up to the challenge.

Chaplain Applicant #20-Yes- three years.

Chaplain Applicant #21-No, but have in the past.

Chaplain Applicant #22-No-moving about. I do not have too many chaplains I would trust.

Chaplain Applicant #23-Yes. Two years.

Chaplain Applicant #24-Yes-my whole life.

Chaplain Applicant #25-At different locations I have had a relationship with someone who has filled this need.

Chaplain Applicant #26- Did not complete question.

Brief Analysis:
Many see the need for a spiritual mentor or director, but often times do not search for one. Why? Chaplain applicant number seventeen answered no and is not looking for a spiritual director or mentor. He could be a potential candidate for compassion fatigue, burnout or other down falls in ministry.

Question #14: Have you ever been a spiritual director or mentor? If so, what did your program consist of?

Chaplain Applicant #1-No.

Chaplain Applicant #2-Not formally.

Chaplain Applicant #3-No.

Chaplain Applicant #4-Yes; however, I had no standardized program / plan. I made myself approachable / available, often acting as nothing more than a sounding board-interjecting occasionally and appropriately. I'd meet with the individual in a relaxing setting usually over a meal.

One of the practices I try to maintain is being there for my family and fellow ministers. While in the church, I told my secretary that even though I was in a counseling session, if my wife, children or a fellow minister called and said they needed to speak to me he was to patch it through. My counselee would just have to accept the interruption. Some may say that's not fair to the counselee; I however, think that it's important to be there for my wife, children and fellow ministers because at that moment they might be in need of spiritual care, prayer, or a swift kick in the backend. I might be the last line of defense before they give way to a temptation that has far reaching morale and ethical consequences.

Chaplain Applicant #5-Yes, but only informally. I mentor through relationship and circumstances.

Chaplain Applicant #6-I'm not sure I have been. My spiritual directors may or may not know that they are. Like most relationships we don't spend time talking about the relationship…it just happens. There is intentionality, but, for me, there has to be an emotionally responsive connection/attachment.

Chaplain Applicant #7-Not a spiritual director, but I have had accountability partners.

Chaplain Applicant #8-No. I have not.

Chaplain Applicant #9-No.

Chaplain Applicant #10-Yes, my program consists of spending a quality time with mentoree. Talking to them and praying with them about their hopes, dreams and aspiration. Calling them, doing innovative and creative activities with them. Can be something as simple as going to a ball game together or attending church together.

Chaplain Applicant #11-Yes, we shared his personal challenges and kept one another accountable regarding self-care and all aspects of ministry and personal / family life.

Chaplain Applicant #12-Loosely defined, I've done a lot of this as a chaplain and chaplain candidate since May 1989.

Chaplain Applicant #13-Yes. Supervised the "chaplain piece" of a CPE-sponsored D.Min. Project for a subordinate chaplain. Consisted of weekly, interdisciplinary team meetings and one-on-one meetings with the individual.

Chaplain Applicant #14-No.

Chaplain Applicant #15-I have been both. As a mentor, I met with younger chaplains on a regular basis according to their needs, some met with me almost daily while others met with me every couple of weeks. As a spiritual director, we met monthly unless otherwise needed.

Chaplain Applicant #16-No.

Chaplain Applicant #17-No.

Chaplain Applicant #18-No, but I'd like to in the future, especially as a Senior Protestant Chaplain.

Chaplain Applicant #19-Not officially; did not use a program.

Chaplain Applicant #20-Yes.

Chaplain Applicant #21-No.

Chaplain Applicant #22-No.

Chaplain Applicant #23-Yes. Time, counsel, activities away from the military, retreats to the ocean, etc.

Chaplain Applicant #24-Yes. Balanced youth program with activities, Soldier "Living a Balanced Life." I tried in Korea I encouraged, but became unbalanced myself.

Chaplain Applicant #25-Yes, as a youth pastor-a denominational curriculum. Also, while pastoring with three men I met weekly for one hour. We went over accountability questions and "Our Daily Bread" daily devotionals.

Chaplain Applicant #26- Did not complete question.

<u>Brief Analysis:</u>

Thirteen chaplain applicants answered 'yes' and ten answered 'no.' The remaining chaplain applicants acted in not in the formal sense of the word spiritual director or mentor, but accountability partners.

Interview One

The chaplain agreed to allow his conversation to be used in my research. He felt there was a tremendous need for him and other chaplain's story of pain to be heard. I assured him that I would not take notes or reveal his name, unit or in anyway that the reader could associate or narrow him down to any particular incident.

The counseling session took place in Kuwait. I was conducting on-call duty which lasted for five days. The main purpose of the duty was to brief all in-bound flight passengers returning from the United States are other areas from two weeks of rest and recuperation (R&R) leave. The focus was to help transition the returning service members from their R&R mentality into reentering a combat theater environment. For some, their R&R was a wonderful time with family and friends, while other's experience was not so pleasant. Normally, the flights would arrive in Kuwait late in the night or early mornings. The service members were jet lagged, trying to make the time change as well as emotional shift. The service members connecting flights to their final destination, to rejoin their unit, ranged from a few hours to a few days. The individuals briefing included the chaplain or chaplain assistant, customs and housing. The chaplain portion of the brief consisted of a welcome, orientation of the chapel, listing of religious activities, such as worship services, bibles studies, etc., and the on-call duty cellular number. Providing the on-call cellular number allowed anyone who needed too seek the chaplain could do so privately, if necessary. I would remain through the entire briefing in case someone wanted to talk. On this particular night no one sought the services of the chaplain, so I returned to my sleeping area. If there was a chaplain and / or a chaplain assistant in one of the flights, I would try to make contact with them to ensure that they were provide a centrally located place to sleep and rest until their connecting flight. One of the chaplain assistants stationed in Kuwait established a mini UMT hotel to help minister to transitioning UMTs. Sometimes we would miss the transitioning UMTs because there was no layover time between flights.

On one particular day, while I was walking near the chapel, I saw a chaplain who was waiting to catch his flight. His flight was going to depart in an hour. We started to talk and after several minutes he shared with me the difficult time he had with himself and his family while on R&R. He expressed often times with tears in his eyes the desire not to return to theater and deal with some of his dilemmas. The main reason is because he was burned-out, which lead him to start questioning his calling in the ministry. This was his second deployment. Several months before going on R&R, he had made an awful moral mistake. He mentioned, while he was broken from ministering to his Soldiers, a female Soldier from another unit sought his counseling. After several counseling sessions, he sensed a mutual attraction between the two of them. He tried to pull away from her and have her see another chaplain for counseling, but he said he felt spiritually weak. He mentioned that he felt there were no other chaplains he could confide in and he thought he could handle the situation. He knew his devotional time with God was declining because of the need to minister to his Soldiers. He states that he minimized his self-care to care for them. He felt his sense of self was lost and his relationship with God was declining. He was working out of spiritual scarcity not spiritual abundance.

He ended up having a sexual relationship with her and became so involved that when she redeployed he spiraled into a deep state of depression. They maintained email and telephonic communications for a while, thus not helping his depression. "How could I be so irresponsible? Can God forgive me? I am a hypocrite! Do I tell my wife? What if others find out?"

He attributed his poor judgment to multiple deployments, no time to recharge his spiritual batteries, overwhelmed to military duties, overlook of counseling and no other chaplain to assist, not having good self-care strategies, perfectionism, being spiritually weak and giving into satan's relentless attacks.

Interview Two

The individual in this interview was a U.S. Army Chaplain for approximately nine years. Before entering the military, he was pastoring and had been for several years successfully. He joined the U.S. Army Chaplaincy for patriotism and for the adventure. During his first assignment, which was a United States Army Training and Doctrine Command (TRADOC) unit, he started questioning if he made the right decision. He enjoyed the ministry to the new entry Soldiers, cadre and their families, but the work load was over bearing. There were also problems of restrictions on worship, promises not being fulfilled and a lack of understanding of the role of a chaplain by the chain of command. Being a chaplain of an initial entry or basic training unit is very tasking. The job of the cadre is to reshape and educate citizens into becoming citizen Soldiers. The trainees, which they are called, are dealing with a multitude of adjustment issues and often seek the chaplain for numerous reasons. Some of the reasons are for spiritual advice, a sounding board and as a means to get discharged from the military for failure to adjust.

For a chaplain to remain in this type of unit the entire term, which was approximately three years is not healthy. In a TRADOC unit the counseling demands are numerous and consistent. During a summer surge when the majority of the classes are filled, the result can mean approximately two thousand trainees for one UMT to provide and perform ministry. The individual in this interview had been in this unit for two to two and a half years. When he was finally moved to a United States Army Forces Command (FORSCOM) unit, he had already experienced symptoms of burnout. In spite of the systemic Army problem of doing more with less, OPTEMPO, unrealistic expectations and time away from family, by God's grace he was able to recover.

The decision to leave the military was a difficult one, but one he does not regret. He learned a lot from military ministry, but chose to reenter the civilian parish. Some of the reasons that he left military ministry were: he felt he had little control over his career, the separation from his family was too much, OPTEMPO, feelings of being overworked and unappreciated, and unrealistic expectations and demands from his command team.

CHAPTER SIX

PASTORAL APPLICATION

Introduction

There is no cookie cutter approach to self-care due to different denominations and the individuality of the chaplain. My intent is to provoke new ideas, offer a fresh perspective, and add to a chaplain's repertoire and pre-existing self-care tool bag. In the area of self-renewal the Chaplain Corps offers the following, but no limited to: Provider Resiliency training, Spiritual Reintegration and Resiliency training, Battle Space Pastoral training, Clinical Pastoral Education (CPE), Eye Movement Desensitization and Reprocessing (EMDR) approach and encourages chaplains to attend their endorsement agency conferences.

Provider Resiliency training instructs the caregiver on the qualities to build resiliency in their lives. Spiritual Reintegration and Resiliency training is designed to help Soldiers and their families develop personal strength and resiliency to overcome hardships, such as combat, deployment separations and adversity. Battle Space Pastoral training is orientated for the chaplain to assist in enhancing their pastoral care skills. EMDR was discovered by Dr. Francine Shapiro in 1987. In the EMDR approach problems and/or issues are viewed as based in unprocessed physiologically stored memories impacting present thoughts, emotions, and behaviors. EMDR approach utilizes eight phases to properly process and store the unprocessed physiologically stored memories. The Chief of Army Chaplains understands that attending denominational conferences and events provides essential opportunities for spiritual development and enhancement of professional skills, thus substantially benefiting the chaplain's performance of duty.

This does not exclude the chaplain corps or the chaplain from being intentional and implementing self-care strategies and training daily, quarterly or annually. From the research, there is a need for some additional guidelines from the Chaplain Corps on self-care. Experience teaches and the yearning of the soul tells us there is a need to conduct self-care. A module of self-care techniques could be implemented during each installations monthly unit ministry team (UMT) training and / or as continuing education credits. The Covenant and Code of Ethics could be displayed periodically in the Chief of Chaplains Newsletter, Chaplain Corps Strategic Campaign Plan, in UMT offices and training tri-folders (Appendix D). It could also be reduced and placed on a wallet size laminated card along with the Chaplain Corps' vision and mission statement. The section of the Chaplain Corps Strategic Campaign Plan, 2008-2013 that mentions including a spiritual development plan in every Chaplain Officer Evaluation Report (OER) Support Form 67-9-1b and conducting annual spiritual development workshops or retreats at institutional level and above for UMT and family members can be reinforced by supervisory chaplains.

The model of self-care is not limited to chaplains, but is applicable for chaplain assistants, administrative assistants, directors of religious education and anyone that works or volunteers for the religious support team. This is a healing ministry model where care must also be given to the caregivers.

Each of us, from time to time, finds ourselves in need of a pit stop, oil change or whatever it takes to recalibrate and refuel. And the point is, we know we need it, but we also know we are not yet able to make it happen. As a result, often we find ourselves feeling stuck.

We have to make a conscious decision to work some self-care into our schedule. We have been made to believe that spiritual fitness is organic, that it's natural. But it's not. It's intentional. It takes effort, force, and planning. Life can not be compared to a romance novel. We're not going to just meet someone wonderful here on this earth who will take care of our every need. That primary caretaker is the one staring at you in the mirror. Chaplains need to practice what they preach.

One of these issues is that the Sabbath Sunday or Lord's Day is not considered a day of rest or worship for chaplains. Many times chaplains are orchestrating the worship services. Chaplains work at least six days a week. The Army states that Soldiers are Soldiers twenty-four hours a day seven days a week. Since a chaplain is employed by the Army the same rule would apply to them as well. The question is posed, "When do chaplains get the appropriate rest they need to care spiritually for themselves, other chaplains, Soldiers and their families they minister to?" Historically, chaplains may or may not get adequate compensation time throughout the week. Many times this does not happen for various reasons. For example, with the many demands of the 'mission,' chaplains must be available in the work place to Soldiers and families. Many chaplains are not comfortable for whatever reasons to establish or designate a compensation day. "Working to the point of exhaustion, without days off or vacations, seems like commendable dedication, but actually, it may be a foolish expenditure of strength."[82] Often chaplains work out of spiritual scarcity and not spiritual abundance. A common quote is, "if we do not care for ourselves, we are not able to provide for others." "If dedicated ministers were to pace themselves, care for their

---

[82] Trull and Carter, 69.

bodies, and guard their health, they would then expand their ministries rather than cut them short by an early death or failing health."[83]

A self-care model is designed to withstand the difficulties and pressures of life. Ultimately, it is God who strengthens us from the adversities and hardships that come into our lives. God must empower us from within or we will be unable to withstand the pressures from the world. The power of Christ within us is greater than the pressure of troubles around us. The self-care model is designed to be used in the normal ebb and flow of ministry.

Proposed Self-Care Model: PAUSE and RELAX (Take A Knee!)

There is an enormous amount of terms used by the military and its agencies. In order to simplify the language, the military uses acronyms. Acronyms are a way to remember a phrase, key points and a lot of information. The following acronym 'PAUSE' and 'RELAX'[84] are ways to illustrate and describe in a short and abbreviated manner the model of self-care. I developed this idea from participating in military field training exercises (FTXs). The FTXs are designed to train, test, modify and correct a unit's fighting ability against actual or simulated opposing forces. FTXs are conducted under simulated combat conditions in the field. The duration of a FTX ranges from days to weeks to months. In between missions, there would be a 'change of mission' or 'endex.' 'Change of mission' simply meant that there was a 'PAUSE' in the action and there was a brief moment to 'RELAX.' It also meant the current mission would change to another mission and the unit would take time to reevaluate and reassess their success or failure in the current mission. During this time, the unit would also ensure they were ready to fight and win in the new mission. They would ensure they had enough personnel to fight the war and logistics to supply the fight. 'Endex' means the unit would end the training exercise. During the 'endex' period, there would be an evaluation period called an after action review (AAR). The observer controller (OC), grader, would guide the unit thorough the AAR. The format of the AAR is: what was your mission, did you accomplish your mission and if you did not, why; what would you do better next time.

Ministry is similar to the units in the FTXs in the way that the caregiver needs to 'PAUSE and RELAX' in order to reevaluate and prepare for ongoing ministry. Another way of viewing this model is the word picture of an athlete 'taking a knee' during a sporting event to catch their breath. Taking a knee is a display of discipline. During football practice or a football game when a time-out is taken the players automatically will take a knee. Taking a knee allows the players to rest momentarily from the sport and to listen to the coach give further instructions without being interrupted.

---

[83] Ibid, 69.
[84] Sermon Title: "God's Antidote To Busyness," 2004.

Taking a knee is also symbolic of kneeling to pray. It is a time of remembering who is in control and that it is not about the chaplain, but God's glory being manifested. The chaplain's best requires spiritual rest. The provider cannot give what they do not possess.

The 'PAUSE and RELAX' can be conducted in the same manner that routine maintenance is applied to military vehicles: Preventive Maintenance Checks and Services (PMCS). Conducting PMCS before, during and after operations ensures one's vehicle or piece of equipment can stay operational and stay in the fight. The chaplain must perform a similar type maintenance on self to ensure they are able to provide quality pastoral care to our nation's service members and their families. The proposed model can be modified to ensure self-care is conducted like a good PMCS before, during and after ministry operations.

This model of self-care can be adapted to the unique needs of each chaplain. Self-care practices result in increasing the spiritual, mental, and physical health and readiness of the chaplaincy, chaplains can take better care of themselves when they learn different self-care techniques to help prevent and treat burnout and / or compassion fatigue. It helps to empower chaplains to be responsible for their spiritual health, sets the example for other helping agencies, chaplaincy staff and command teams, it reduces the ministry time lost by chaplains trying to recover from fatigue and depression and reduces with the goal of eliminating the number of untimely deaths.

Chaplains are not alone in their struggle to avoid becoming fragmented and their quest for spiritual renewal. The Prophet Elijah experienced burnout in ministry. In 1 Kings 19:1-10, God fed the despondent prophet Elijah with heavenly food. The lesson to take from these scriptures is God is with us in our most barren wilderness. An unquenched spirit feels as if it is in a barren wilderness. In the Bible, the wilderness is often the setting for the mighty work of God within the human heart. In our wilderness experience, God can and will teach us lessons of endurance and faith. These are valuable lessons one would never learn in a busy life.

On commercial airlines, during flights the flight attendant will conduct a safety brief. Part of the safety brief is the illustration of how to put on the oxygen mask. They instruct the passengers to first mask themselves then mask the person next to them and / or a small child. The reason for this is if you have no oxygen you will hyperventilate and panic. Then you will be no good to anyone. This metaphor is applicable to the spiritual life of the chaplain. The chaplain must be able to mask themselves properly before assisting others to mask. In other words, the chaplain must conduct self-care to ensure they maintain spiritual sanity not succumb to spiritual suffocation. This model by no means is exhaustive. One may want to amplify the model and add more of their own self-care strategies.

While deployed I taught an abbreviated portion of the self-care model to a group of lay ministers. The lay members consisted of active duty, National Guard, and reserve component Soldiers, and Department of Defense employees, which some had retired from military service. Their comments after the training were very positive. They greatly appreciated the training, were amazed with the research and shared their negative experiences of being overcome by overloaded in ministry. Those that attended the training their ministerial experienced ranged from working in youth ministry, being an associate minister, in the journey of answering their calling into the Gospel ministry, and having experience as a pastor. The participant's years in ministry ranged from months to twenty years.

Listed below is a brief quiz to score if a person is a work-a-holic in need of spiritual renewal.

Work-A-Holic Quiz

1. Are you always in a hurry?
2. Do you establish unrealistic goals for yourself?
3. Is your 'To Do List' entirely too long?
4. In order to take a day off from work do you have to be sick?
5. How many annual leave days have you lost?

If you answer 'yes' to any of the questions you are in need to 'take a knee,' practice the 'pause' and to 'relax' model.

PAUSE

P-Praise.

Praise is the missing ingredient in the life of someone who registers negative in the spiritual renewal department. Praise is remembering what God has done previously in the caregiver's life. The caregiver can list the ways God has cared for them in the past, and how He has provided for them or answered many prayer requests. Praise is remembering God's promises despite the caregiver's current circumstances and thanking God for the victory. "Be strong and of good courage for the Lord your God is with you wherever you go." (Joshua 1:9) Like David (1 Samuel 30:6), let's learn to strengthen ourselves in the Lord, and then let's leave the rest with Him.

The Psalmist (Psalm 46: 1-11) offers comforting words that spending quiet time with God will bring quiet rest from God. For the chaplain, undisturbed stillness has become more elusive and therefore more necessary than ever to seek. In the fast-paced world of the chaplain, they need to be still and acknowledge that God is in charge. A respite from activity allows one to focus their thoughts on the majesty of God. God is greater than any personal pressures.

Psalm 46:10, "Be still (cease striving), and know that I am God; I will be exalted among the nations, I will be exalted in the earth."

Be still/cease striving is the Hebrew word *"Raphah."* The root is to 'sink' or 'relax.' Raphah suggests relying on God's strength instead of our own.

Psalm 150:1-2, 6, "Praise the Lord. Praise God in His sanctuary; praise Him in His mighty heavens. Praise Him for His acts of power; praise Him for His surpassing greatness. Let everything that has breath praise the Lord. Praise the Lord.

A-**Awareness.**

Awareness of emotional, physical, and spiritual status; theological reflection is valuable time to reflect on the day's events from a biblical perspective. Avoid reliving traumatic incidents, the patient's pain and your pain. Being aware of our emotional status allows us to have the faith of a new vision, the freedom to let go of the past, giving strength to embrace the present.

Mark 6:31 states, "Then, because so many people were coming and going that they did not even have a chance to eat, he said to them, 'Come with me by your selves to a quiet place and get some rest.'"

Matthew 13:1 states, "That same day Jesus went out of the house and sat by the lake." The periscope does not disclose Jesus specific actions by the lake other than sitting by it. But with some biblical imagination His actions illustrate His awareness of His need to be alone. This self-renewal behavior was temporary, but a natural part of Jesus ministry. Jesus did not conduct ministry when he was tired.

U-**Urgency.**

During a crisis identify the urgency of the need for pastoral care. The challenge for the caregiver is to find their sacred rhythm in the OPTEMPO of the military. Too often chaplains live captive to the demands of ministry. Jesus moved with a sense of urgency and practice power to control the pace of his responses to ministry. During the death of Lazarus (John 11:1-44), Jesus was fully engaged in the moment but, he did not allow the crisis of that grief disturb his pace to Calvary. He was on pace to complete his Father's business. Jesus practice of pace control during perilous circumstances allowed him to move with passion despite the oppressive rhythm of the moment. While at sea, Jesus was awaking by the disciples due to fear of the devastating storm (Mark 4:35-41). Once awake, Jesus was able to assess the disciple's request and to prioritize the urgency; Jesus need of rest was accomplished and the storm calmed. It is amazing what Jesus accomplished after a nap!

In Psalm 1, there is no hint of a frenzied pace. It describes a person who enjoys the blessing of God. Instead of thinking and acting like those who rarely consider spiritual matters, "His delight is in the law of the Lord, and in His law meditates day and night" (v.2). The result is a fruitful life and a well-nourished soul (v.3).

Isaiah wrote, "You will keep Him in perfect peace, whose mind is stayed on you, because He trusts in you" (Isaiah 26:3).

S- Sabbath Rest.

Sabbath means a day of rest. Exodus 20:9-10 highlights this Sabbath day of rest. God gives permission to stop and do nothing; to cease, embrace and feast. The Mosaic code for the Sabbath used a six to one model: six days of work and one day of Sabbath rest. For the chaplaincy, I propose a five to two model: five days of work with one day of Sabbath rest (Saturday) and another day for worship (Sunday). In turn, the five to two model is really a six to one model. Sunday is a day of worship, but it can also be considered a day of work because the chaplain is leading the worship service or involved in some way that takes them away from properly celebrating the Lord's Day with rest.

Sabbath can be defined as, "to cease, desist, the weekly day of rest and abstention from work."[85] An individual day of Sabbath rest and worship will assist one in the journey of reaching wholeness versus being fragmented.

Mark 2:27 states, "Then he said to them, The Sabbath was made for man, not man for the Sabbath." What do you do on the Sabbath? First, rest your body. Secondly, recharge your emotions. For example, time alone, recreation, relationship with people and not always talking work are ways to recharge. Lastly, refocus your spirit. Refreshing one's spirit can be completed through individual worship and corporate worship. Consider making a spare room in your house or space in your office into a sanctuary. People spend a great deal of time and money on television rooms specific for watching television, why not make one for communing with God? This is a time to commune with God and gain peace within. Consider establishing a faith community, which includes a spiritual director or mentor in the life of the chaplain. The benefits are outstanding!

E-Escape.

Escape to find some solitude. Create a regular, non-negotiable place in your schedule that is solely for the purpose of being alone and still before God. Enjoy life and the moment, find joy in your situation, and escape the moment to withdrawal from unwelcoming times. Undisturbed stillness has become more elusive and therefore, more necessary than ever to seek. Jesus made a practice of withdrawing to the wilderness to pray and receive direction (Mark 1:35). If chaplains do not isolate themselves and rest a while, they may just unravel.

The Psalmist (127:2) states, "In vain you rise early and stay up late, toiling for food to eat—for he grants sleep to those he loves.

---

[85] Paul J. Achtemeier, Harper's Bible Dictionary. (San Francisco: HarperCollins Publishers, 1985), 888.

The Psalmist (23: 2 and 3) instructs us to get rest, refreshment and restoration for our soul, "He makes me lie down in green pastures, He leads me beside quiet waters, He restores my soul."

In order to get this peace and quiet, perhaps chaplains need a sabbatical. This is different from the thirty days of ordinary leave that the military offers annually. Sabbatical is a period of self-recovery from traumatic events, a time away from busyness. Perhaps, the chaplaincy can learn more from our civilian pastor counterparts about sabbaticals. Civilian clergy are more likely able to take a two to three month sabbatical. In the U.S. Army that amount of time is not a reality. Solitude, the withdrawal from people in order to get some rest in a secluded quiet place is a must for sabbatical retreats. Matthew 14:13 illustrates this point, "When Jesus heard what had happened, he withdrew by boat privately to a solitary place."

RELAX

R- Realize your worth.

God is far more interested in what we are than what we do. "For God so loved the world that he gave his one and only Son…(John 3:16)" "Look at the birds of the air; they do not sow or reap or store away in barns, and yet your heavenly Father feeds them. Are you not much more valuable than they? (Matthew 6:26)" (cp. Luke 15:1-7; Isaiah 49:16; James 1:8)

John 10:10 provides these words of Jesus, "The thief comes only to steal and kill and destroy; I have come that they may have life, and have it to the full." "Greater is He that is in me than he that is in the world" (1 John 4:4). The power of Christ within you is greater than the pressure of troubles around you. Avoid negative self-criticism at all cost. Negative self-criticism limits one's ability to develop a satisfying life.

E-Enjoy what God has already giving you.

Ecclesiastes 3:13 states, "That everyone may eat and drink, and find satisfaction in all his toil-this is the gift of God." (cp. Ecclesiastes 4:6) Enjoy what God has already giving you. Omit the desire to acquire. Learn to model the Apostle Paul's illustration of contentment. (Appendix C; cp. Philippians 4:4-13 and 1 Timothy 6:5-7)

Proverbs 17:22 states, "Laughter is like a good medicine." In the word "time" is a smaller word that tends to get overlooked: "me." That's right, "me." It's okay to think about yourself for a minute. Often in our lives we become so harried by jobs and family life that we forget to take "me time." "Me time" can consist of a hobby or once a month treat yourself to a solo night out at the movies or any other event. One way to view this is to date yourself. If the chaplain keeps filling out withdrawal slips and no deposit slips from the bank they will start receiving statements of 'non-sufficient funds.' Another way to view it is if the chaplain keeps drawing from the water reservoir it will soon go dry if it is not replaced. John 10:10 states, "I have come that you may have life more abundantly."

L-Limit your labor.

Ecclesiastes 10:15 states, "A fool's work wearies him…" Limit your labor and manage your stress. The removal of stress is not automatic. It is the cooperative effort of the chaplain and God. Our best requires rest! Spending quiet time with God will bring quiet rest from God. A respite from activity allows us to focus our thoughts on the majesty of God. In our fast-paced world, we need to be still and acknowledge that God is in charge (cp. Psalm 46:1-11). Busyness hinders one's relationship with God and cripples one's ministry to others. Jesus is our pace setter. Remember, "The Sabbath was made to benefit man not man for the Sabbath" (Mark 2:27).

A-Adjust your values.

Ecclesiastes 4:4 states, "And I saw that all labor and all achievement spring from man's envy of his neighbor. This too is meaningless, a chasing after the wind." (cp. Mark 8:36; 1 Timothy 6:6-8) Nurture yourself more. Reduce the physical, emotional and spiritual fatigue. Establish a hobby. Hobbies, vacations, and wholesome recreation are vital to a well-balanced, godly life. The caregiver cannot do their work with nerves taut or frayed from constant pressure. The chaplains lose their effectiveness by keeping their lives so tightly strung that they are always tense. If it seems we can't relax, Jesus may be inviting us to adjust our values to take a break to 'come aside and rest a while' (cp. Mark 6:31; Luke 9:1-10). "Unless the Lord builds the house, its builders labor in vain…" (Psalm 127:1).

X-Exchange your pressure for God's peace.

The pressures of life and vocation could be self imposed. Remember that God is in charge. Exchange your pressure for God's peace. We can take comfort in knowing that and allowing God to take our heavy yoke (Matthew 11:25-30) and burdens.

Matthew 11: 28-29, "Come to me, all you that are carrying heavy burdens, and I will give you rest. Take my yoke upon you, and learn from me; for I am gentle and humble in heart, and you will find rest for your souls."

Hebrews 12:1-3 highlights the point of exchange:

> v.1 Therefore we also, since we are surrounded by so great a cloud of witnesses, let us lay aside every weight, and the sin which so easily ensnares us, and let us run with endurance the race that is set before us, v.2 looking unto Jesus, the author and finisher of our faith, who for the joy that was

set before Him endured the cross, despising the shame, and has sat down at the right hand of he throne of God. v.3 For consider Him who endured such hostility from sinners against Himself, lest you become weary and discouraged in your souls.

Conclusion

The model of PAUSE and RELAX is designed not to be a difficult model, but one that can be used daily. It can be used in the midst of providing ministry. The benefits of PAUSE and RELAX model incorporated with a wholesome meal plan and exercise regiment are endless.

From a Christian perspective, the Holy Spirit works to strengthen us and renew our minds as we read the Bible and pray. If we neglect the Scriptures, seldom talk with the Lord, and stop fellowshipping with other believers, we'll grow weak and vulnerable. Then we will be unable to withstand the pressures of temptation or trouble. Ephesians 3:16, speaks on inner strength, "I pray that out of His glorious riches, He may strengthened you with power through His Spirit in your inner being." Remember to 'take a knee' during exhausting days. Practice the 'pause' and 'relax' when your soul needs to be replenished during persistent conflict.

God is a God of all comfort and freely provides this resource. Saint Paul in 2 Corinthians 1:3-4 reminds us of this, "Praise be to God and Father of our Lord Jesus Christ, the Father of compassion and the God of all comfort, who comfort us in all our troubles, so that we can comfort those in any trouble with the comfort we ourselves have received from God." God comforts the chaplain during their time of healing and renewal as they are conduits of comfort and hope for those they minister to.

PRE-TEST QUESTIONNAIRE

Questionnaire on Self-Care[86]

Rank:
Years in service as Chaplain:
Means to contact you for later reference:

1) State your self-care techniques.

2) What is the Chaplain's Corp history of self-care? (i.e. formal or informal)

---

[86] Self-care defined: The acknowledgement of who one is spiritually, mentally, and physically, and the care needed to maintain effective job performance and holistic wellness.

3) Have you experienced burnout[87]? If so, why? Do you know of anyone who has experienced burnout? If so, what were the causes?

3a) If you have experienced burnout, what type of help did you seek if any? If assistance was sought, did you maintain or improve your self-care techniques?

3b) In your opinion, evaluate the Chaplain Corps emphasis on self-care.

4) In your experience what does burnout look like?

5) Define self-care in your own language.

6) What civilian clergy self-care techniques (i.e. denominational) did you bring into the Chaplain Corp?

---

[87] Burnout defined: A temporary disability that prevents one from effective job performance.

7) How do you conduct and how have you conducted self-care during garrison, FTX, peacekeeping operations, and combat deployments?

8) Is there a need for a formal self-care module and/or program in the Chaplain Corp?

9) Are you and other Chaplains following the Covenant and Code of Ethics for Chaplains of the Armed Forces?[88]

10) Do you have a spiritual director or mentor (military or civilian)? If so, how long have you had one? If not, why?

11) Have you ever been a spiritual director or mentor? If so, what did your program consist of?

---

[88] A project of the National Conference on Ministry to the Armed Forces, February 2003. "I will maintain a disciplined ministry in such ways as keeping hours of prayer and devotion, endeavoring to maintain wholesome family relationships, and regularly engaging in educational and recreational activities for professional and personal development. I will seek to maintain good health habits."

QUESTIONNAIRE

Questionnaire on Self-Care[89]

Name:
Rank:
Years in service as a Chaplain:
Denominational Affiliation:
Marital Status:
Number of children:
Number of CPE units completed:
Nationality/Ethnic background:
Number of Deployments (Peacekeeping/Combat):
Means to contact you for later reference:

1) State your self-care techniques.

2) What is the Chaplain's Corp history of self-care? (i.e. formal or informal)

---

[89] Self-care defined: The acknowledgement of who one is spiritually, mentally, and physically, and the care needed to maintain effective job performance and holistic wellness.

3) Have you experienced burnout[90]?

3a) If so, why?

4) Do you know of anyone who has experienced burnout?

4a) If so, what were the causes?

5) If you have experienced burnout, what type of help did you seek if any?

5b) If assistance was sought, did you maintain or improve your self-care techniques?

---

[90] Burnout defined: A temporary disability that prevents one from effective job performance.

6) In your opinion, evaluate the Chaplain Corps emphasis on self-care.

7) In your experience what does burnout look like or identify some indicators of burnout?

8) Define self-care in your own language.

9) What civilian clergy self-care techniques (i.e. denominational) did you bring into the Chaplain Corp?

10) How do you conduct and how have you conducted self-care during garrison, FTX, peacekeeping operations, and combat deployments?

11) Is there a need for a formal self-care module and/or program in the Chaplain Corp?

12) Are you and other Chaplains following the Covenant and Code of Ethics for Chaplains of the Armed Forces?[91]

13) Do you have a spiritual director or mentor (military or civilian)? If so, how long have you had one? If not, why?

14) Have you ever been a spiritual director or mentor? If so, what did your program consist of?

---

[91] A project of the National Conference on Ministry to the Armed Forces, February 2003. "I will maintain a disciplined ministry in such ways as keeping hours of prayer and devotion, endeavoring to maintain wholesome family relationships, and regularly engaging in educational and recreational activities for professional and personal development. I will seek to maintain good health habits."

APPENDIX C

CONTENTMENT

Contentment means sufficiency (verb, 1 Timothy 6:8), self-sufficient (adjective, Philippians 4:2), and satisfaction with what one has (noun, 1 Timothy 6:6). It is that disposition of mind in which one is, through grace, independent of outward circumstances.[92]

Contentment is found in union with Christ. Paul (Philippians 4:4-13) instructs God's people to find contentment, especially in suffering. Contentment is subjective.

Paul is the author of this letter to the Philippians. It is evident that he wrote the letter from prison (1:13-14). Paul's primary purpose in writing this letter was to thank the Philippians for the gift they had sent him upon learning of his detention at Rome (1:5; 4:10-19). However, he makes use of this occasion to fulfill several other desires: (1) to report on his own circumstances (1:12-26 and 4:10-19); (2) to encourage the Philippians to stand firm in the face of persecution and rejoice regardless of circumstances (1:27-30 and 4:4); (3) to exhort them to humility and unity (2:1-11 and 4:2-5); (4) to commend Timothy and Epaphroditus to the Philippian church (2:19-30); and (5) to warn the Philippians against the Judaizers (legalists) and antinomians (libertines) among them (chapter 3).

Paul's first desire for the Christian is to maintain a spirit of joy in the Lord (v.4). 1 Thessalonians 5:16 reiterates this point, "Be joyful always." Paul's second desire is to encourage the Philippians to stand firm in the face of persecution and rejoice regardless of circumstances.

Paul proceeds to exhort the church to maintain certain positive Christian virtues. First, believers are to "rejoice in the Lord always" and "again" to "rejoice." The double emphasis on rejoicing may imply that a single injunction might prompt the question "How can we rejoice, in view of our difficulties?" So he repeats the command, because in all the virtues of the Christian life, whether in attacks from errorists, personality clashes among believers, persecution from the world, or threat of imminent death-all of which Paul himself was experiencing at this very time-the Christians is to maintain a spirit of joy in the Lord. He or she is not immune to sorrow nor should they be insensitive to the troubles of others;

---

[92] Merrill F. Unger, <u>The New Unger's Bible Dictionary.</u> (Chicago: Moody Press, 1988), 254.

yet they should count the will of God their highest joy and so be capable of knowing inner peace and joy in every circumstance. Contentment is not getting what we want but being satisfied with what we have.

There is an old saying that goes, "that is easy for you to say." One might think that it was easy for Paul to say such a thing. But he was speaking to the Philippian Church and to us today from house arrest. Remember Paul experienced server beatings, he was stoned, shipwrecked, hungry and thirsty, left half dead, cold and naked, and persecuted (2 Corinthians 11: 23-28). He was even beheaded.

Christians are to always rejoice under all kinds of circumstances, including suffering. How is it that Christians can rejoice? James 1:2-4, "Consider it pure joy, my brothers, whenever you face trials of many kinds, because you know that the testing of your faith develops perseverance. Perseverance must finish its work so that you may be mature and complete, not lacking anything."

> 1 Peter 4: 12 -14, 19, "Dear friends, do not be surprised at the painful trial you are suffering, as though something strange were happening to you. But rejoice that you participate in the sufferings of Christ, so that you may be overjoyed when his glory is revealed. If you are insulted because of the name of Christ, you are blessed, for the Spirit of glory and of God rests on you. So then, those who suffer according to God's will should commit themselves to their faithful Creator and continue to do good."

From Paul's experiences several contentment strategies can be adopted into a person's spiritual life. Daily scripture reading and prayers are a vital key to help facilitate contentment. Do not worry, but pray about everything. The peace of God will cover you as you pray and trust in God. Daily prayer brings one to a Godly focus. Prayer will bring one more peace. For the Christian finding strength is through Christ.

TRI-FOLDER

1. What is self-care- self-care is the acknowledgment of who one is spiritually, mentally, and physically (soul, mind, and body), and the care needed to maintain effectiveness in all areas.

   - Self-care is a natural basic part of life survival.
   - Failing to conduct wellness often leads to disastrous situations.
   - Self-care is a preventative measure, towards holistic wellness.
   - Self-care is an individual responsibility, as well as, the responsibility of the organization.
   - Self-care is practicing prevention and taking personal responsibility for one's own health.
   - Self-care is a balance.

2. Self-Care goals- To ensure the chaplain is spiritually fit to minister to his or her unit Soldiers and their families, congregation, staff, and other UMTs.

3. Self-Care benefits are:

   - Build awareness among military leadership.
   - Combat Multiplier.
   - Establishes boundaries by knowing one's strengthens and limitations.
   - Healthier chaplain physically, mentally, and spiritually.
   - Increases the spiritual health and readiness of the force (U.S. Army).
   - Quality time with family and friends.
   - Builds Spiritual Resiliency.
   - Strengthen the spiritual life of the U.S. Army Chaplain Corps.
   - John 10:10, "I have come that you may have life more abundantly."

4. Model of Self-Care: PAUSE and RELAX (Take a Knee!)

P-**Praise.**, Psalm 46:10
A-**Awareness of emotional, physical, and spiritual status.**, Mark 6: 31
U-**Urgency.**, Psalm 1
S- **Sabbath Rest.**, Mark 2:27
E-**Escape to find some Solitude.**, Psalmist 23: 2 and 3

R-**Realize your worth.**, John 3:16
E-**Enjoy what God has already giving you.**, Ecclesiastes 3:13; 4:6; 1 Timothy 6:6
L-**Limit your labor.**, Ecclesiastes 10:15
A-**Adjust my values.**, Mark 8:36
X-**Exchange your pressure for God's peace**., Matthew 11:25-30

- Celebrate one day per week as Sabbath.
- Challenge cultural beliefs.
- Health-diet and exercise.
- Journaling.
- Manage expectations.
- Manage stress. The removal of stress is not automatic. It is the unified effort of the chaplain and God.
- Set aside time each day for devotion, play, relaxation, and reading.
- Set boundaries.
- Socialization or fellowship.
- Support groups: family, friends, co-workers, prayer partner, spiritual director, and mentor.
- Take momentary respites throughout workday (Practice the 'PAUSE' and 'RELAX').

5. Enemies of self-care: When chaplains do not conduct self-care they minimize their relationship with God, self, family, and the people they minister to.

- Blurred pastoral identity.
- Burnout.
- Compassion fatigue.
- Depersonalization.
- Difficult Supervisory Relationships.
- Emotional exhaustion.
- Environment.
- Hurry.
- Inadequate exercise regiments.
- Losing annual leave.

- Missing vacations.
- Overload.
- Over-functioning vs. Under-functioning.
- Perfectionism.
- Poor dietary meal plans.
- Reduced personal accomplishment.
- Self.
- Sheer number of expectations, variety, unrealistic, and changing nature of expectations from others.
- Stress.
- Time.

6. Work-A-Holic Quiz:

1. Are you always in a hurry?
2. Do you establish unrealistic goals for yourself?
3. Is your 'To Do List' entirely too long?
4. In order to take a day off from work do you have to be sick?
5. How many annual leave days have you lost?

If you answer 'yes' to any other the questions you are in need to 'take a knee,' practice the 'pause' and to 'relax' model.

APPENDIX E

ACRONYMS, ABBREVIATIONS, AND DEFINITION OF TERMS[93]

- After Action Review (AAR)-is a method of providing feedback to units by involving participants in the training diagnostic process in order to increase and reinforce learning.

- Basic Training-is initial military training for new Soldiers.

- Battalion (BN)-has three to five companies in addition to their headquarters. They are organized by branch and can perform some administrative and logistic services.

- Brigade (BDE)-control two or more battalions.

- Clinical Pastoral Education (CPE)-the course is designed to prepare a chaplain to provide pastoral care in a clinical setting.

- Combat Deployment-Soldiers, units, and support agencies deploy from home stations or installations to potential areas of hostilities.

- Doctor of Ministry (D. Min.)-is a terminal degree. The D. Min. is designed to contribute to the theory and practice of ministry within a given pastoral discipline in light of one's own denominational theology.

- Field Training Exercise (FTX)-a high-cost, high-overhead exercise conducted under simulated combat conditions in the field. It exercises command and control of all echelons in battle functions against actual or simulated opposing forces.

---

[93] FM 100-5 Operations, Headquarters, Department of the Army, May 1986.

- United States Army Forces Command (FORSCOM)-manages the deployable armed forces.

- Garrison-a permanent military installation or military post.

- Global War On Terrorism (GWOT)-global fight against foreign and domestic terrorism.

- Installation-a military camp, fort, or base.

- Non Applicable (N/A)-something does not apply.

- Noncommissioned Officer (NCO)-the NCOs have been called "the backbone of the Army." NCOs are tremendously important to the Army; within them, a unit functions like a smooth running machine. Matters in their purview, but limited to are supervision of unit operations, care of individual Soldiers and their families, proper wearing of the uniform, appearance and courtesy of enlisted personnel, care of arms and equipment, care of living quarters, area maintenance tasks, and operation of recreational and other facilities.

- Observer Controller (OC)-an individual tasked to evaluate training, and providing administrative control and constructive feedback to participants during a training exercise.

- Officer Evaluation Report (OER)-is the system of evaluation ratings and periodic reports on the performance of duty of each officer of the Army.

- Officer Rank Structure-Second Lieutenant, First Lieutenant, Captain, Major, Lieutenant Colonel, Colonel, Brigadier General, Major General, Lieutenant General, and General

- Operation Tempo (OPTEMPO)-the annual operating miles or hours for the major equipment system in a battalion-level or equivalent organization. Commanders use OPTEMPO to forecast and allocate funds for fuel and repair parts for training events and programs.

- Peacekeeping Operations-Soldiers, units, and support agencies deploy from home stations or installations to potential hostile areas to establish or reinforce peace.

- Permanent Change of Station (PCS)-is a change in duty assignment.

- Physical Training (P.T.)-is composed of components (cardio-respiratory endurance, muscular strength, muscular endurance, and flexibility) that allow Soldiers to function effectively in physical and mental work, training, and recreation and still have energy to handle emergencies.

- Physician's Assistant (PA)-a person skilled in the art of healing who assist a doctor of medicine.

- Post Traumatic Stress Disorder (PTSD)-the person experienced, witnessed or was confronted with an event or events that involved actual or threatened death or serious injury, or a threat to the physical integrity of self or others.

- Preventive Maintenance Checks and Services (PMCS)-prescribed maintenance procedures found in an operator-level, item-specific technical manual (TM-10), and performed by the operator before, during, and after operating a piece of equipment.

- Rest and Recuperation (R&R)-is a program that allows Soldiers to recover from training or deployments. The intent is to increase morale.

- Stand To-a full alert posture normally assumed from thirty minutes before until thirty minutes after beginning of morning nautical twilight (BMNT) and end of evening nautical twilight (EENT). All Soldiers are in their fighting positions or vehicles and ready for combat operations.

- United States Army Training and Doctrine Command (TRADOC)-is responsible for the establishment of training and writing Army doctrine.

- Training Support Plan (TSP)-the method used to identify forces and equipment needed to support a planned training event.

- Troop Medical Clinic (TMC)-is a health clinic that manages and provides are care to soldiers and their families.

- United States Air Force (USAF)-maintains air superiority for the U.S.

- Unit Ministry Team (UMT)-consist of a chaplain and chaplain assistant. The mission of the UMT is to provide military religious support to Soldiers, families, and authorized civilians as directed by the commander.[94]

---

[94] Religious Support Handbook for the Unit Ministry Team, TC 1-05, headquarters Department of the Army, May 2005.

BIBLIOGRAPHY

Adam, A.K.A. <u>What is Postmodern Biblical Criticism?</u> Minneapolis: Fortress, 1995.

Achtemeier, Paul, J. <u>Harper's Bible Dictionary.</u> San Francisco: HarperCollins Publishers, 1985.

Alonso Schokel, Luis. "Hermeutics in the Light of Language and Literature." <u>Catholic Biblical Quarterly</u> vol. 25 (1963): 371-386.

Anderson, Richard, G. <u>The Fourth Commandment: The Foundation for Self-Care</u>, CPE Pastoral Project. Walter Reed Army Medical Center, 2004.

Barclay, William. <u>The Ten Commandments</u>, 2d ed. Louisville: Westminster John Knox Press, 1998.

Boys, Mary C. and Thomas G. Groome. "Principles and Pedagogy in Biblical Study." <u>Religious Education</u> vol. 77 (Sep-Oct 1982): 486-705.

Berry, Carmen Renee. <u>When Helping You Is Hurting Me</u>. New York: Crossroad Publishing Company, 2003.

Bray, Gerald. <u>Biblical Interpretation-Past and Present</u>. Downers Grove, IL: InterVarsity, 1996.

Briner, Bob and Pritchard, Ray. <u>The Leadership Lessons of Jesus.</u> Broadman and Holman Publishers, Nashville, Tennessee, 1997.

Burgess, John P. <u>Why Scripture Matters: Reading the Bible in a Time of Church Conflict.</u> Louisville: Westminter John Knox, 1998.

Burner, Victoria, "Didatic: Compassion Fatigue." Deployment Health Clinical Center, Walter Reed Army Medical Center, Washington, D.C., 2003-2004.

Cash, LT. Carey H. <u>A Table In The Presence</u>. W. Publishing Group, Nashville, Tennessee, 2004.

Chisnall, Peter, M. "Questionnaire Design, Interviewing and Attitude Measurement." <u>Journal of the Market Research Society</u> vol. 35 (1992): 303.

"Quick Reference to the Diagnostic Criteria from Diagnostic and Statistical Manual of Mental Disorders, Fourth Edition." Washington, D.C.: American Psychiatric Association, 1994.

Drazin, Israel and Currey, Cecil B. FOR GOD AND COUNTRY: The History Of A Constitutional Challenge To The Army Chaplaincy. KTAV Publishing House, Inc., Hoboken, New Jersey, 1995.

Department of the Army. Army Regulation 165-1, Religious Activities: Chaplain Activities in the United States Army. Washington, D.C.: Government Printing Office, 1998.

Department of the Army. TC 1-05, Religious Support Handbook for the Unit Ministry Team. Washington, D.C.: Government Printing Office, 2005.

Eyer, Richard C. Pastoral Care Under The Cross. Concordia Publishing House, St. Louis, MO., 1994.

Eyer, Stephen, The Discipleship Series, Spiritual Disciplines. Zondervan Publishing House: Grand Rapids, Michigan, 1992.

Farstad, Arthur, L. "We Believe: Jesus Is Lord," Journal of the Grace Evangelical Society 2. Spring 1989.

Faulkner, Brooks, R. Burnout in Ministry. Broadman Press, Nashville, Tennessee, 1981.

Friedman, Edwin, H. Generation to Generation: Family Process in Church and Synagogue. New York and London: The Guilford Press, 1985.

Fruchtenbaum, Arnold G. Israelology: Part 1 of 6. Chafer Theological Seminary Journal, 1999.

Gales, Alvester, "Didatic: Trauma Ministry" Clinical Pastoral Education Department, Walter Reed Army Medical Center, Washington, D.C., 2003.

Gladwell, Malcom, Blink: The Power of Thinking Without Thinking. New York: Little, Brown and Company, 2005.

Hagen, Kenneth, ed., The Bible in the Churches. How Various Christians Interpret the Scriptures. 2nd ed. Milwaukee: Marquette University: 1994.

Hare Douglas, R.A., Interpretation of Matthew: A Bible Commentary for Teaching and Preaching. John Knox Press, Louisville, 1993.

Haugk, Kenneth, C. Antagonist in the Church. Minneapolis: Augsburg Publishing House, 1988.

Henrichsen, Walter, A. <u>Disciples are Made not Born: How to help others grow to maturity in Christ.</u> Colorado, Springs, CO: Cook Communication Ministries, 1988.

Henry, Matthew, <u>Commentary On the Whole Bible: Genesis to Deuteronomy, Volume 1.</u> Peabody, MA: Hendrickson Publisher's, 1992.

Henry, Matthew, <u>Commentary On the Whole Bible: Acts to Revelation, Volume 6.</u> Peabody, MA: Hendrickson Publisher's, 1992.

Hicks, H. Beecher, Jr. <u>Preaching Through A Storm.</u> Grand Rapids, M.I.: Zondervan Publishing House, 1987.

The Holy Bible. New International Version.

Jones, Kirk Byron. <u>Rest In the Storm: Self-Care Strategies for Clergy and Other Caregivers.</u> Judson Press, Valley Forge, PA, 2001.

Kinast, Robert. <u>What Are They Saying About Theological Reflection?.</u> New York: Paulist Press, 2000.

Kroll, Jerome. <u>PTSD/Borderlines in Therapy.</u> W.W. Norton and Company, Inc. 1993.

Mansfield, Stephen. <u>The Faith of George W. Bush.</u> Tarcher/Penguin Group (USA) Inc., New York, N.Y., 2003.

Maslach, Christina. <u>Burnout: The Cost of Caring.</u> Malor Books, Cambridge, MA., 2003.

<u>Matthew Henry's Commentary on the Whole Bible</u> vol.5, Hendrickson Publishers, Inc. 1991.

May, James, L. <u>Harper's Bible Commentary.</u> HarperSanFrancisco. 1988.

McGee-Cooper, Ann. <u>You Don't Have To Go Home From Work Exhausted!</u> Bantam Books, New York, N.Y., 1992

Megivern, James J. <u>The Death Penalty: A Historical and Theological Survey.</u> Mahwah, NJ: Paulist, 1997.

Merton, Robert, K. and Kendall Patricia, L. "The Focused Interview." <u>The American Journal of Sociology</u> vol. 51 (1946): 541-557.

Mawhinney, Bruce. <u>Preaching With Freshiness.</u> Grand Rapids, MI: Kregel Publications, 1997.

McGee, Robert S. <u>The Search for Significance.</u> Rapha, Houston, Texas, 1990.

Moore, Thomas. <u>Care of the Soul.</u> HarperCollins, 1994.

Myers, William R. <u>Research in Ministry: A Primer for the Doctor of Ministry Program.</u> Chicago: Exploration Press, 1993.

<u>New International Version Bible.</u> Zondervan Publishing House, Grand Rapids, Michigan, 1984.

Nichols, Michael P. <u>The Lost Art of Listening.</u> Guilford Publications, New York, New York, 1995.

Oates, Wayne, E. <u>Behind the Masks: Personality Disorders in Religious Behavior.</u> Westminister Press, Louisville, Kentucky, 1987.

Palmer, Richard E. Chapter 13, "Toward Reopening the Question: What is Interpretation." Chapter 14, "Thirty Theses on Interpretation." <u>Hermeneutics.</u> Northwestern U. Press 1969. 223-253.

Packer, J.I. <u>Knowing God</u>. InterVarsity Press 1993.

Peterson, Eugene H. <u>Working the Angles: The Shape of Pastoral Integrity.</u> Grand Rapids: William B. Eerdmans Publishing Company, 1987.

"A Project of the National Conference on Ministry to the Armed Forces," February 2003.

Radio Bible College (RBC) Ministries, <u>Our Daily Bread,</u> 9 September 2003.

Rassieur, Charles, L. <u>Career Burnout Prevention Among Pastoral Counselors and Pastors: In Handbook for Basic Types of Pastoral Care and Counseling</u>, ed. Howard W. Stone and William M. Clements, 256-272. Nashville: Abingdon, 1991.

Rediger, G. Lloyd. <u>Coping With Clergy Burnout.</u> Valley Forge, PA: Judson Press, 1982.

Reference Book 16-100. <u>The Unit Ministry Team Handbook.</u> Washington, D.C.: Government Printing Office, January, 1998.

Robin, Theodore I. <u>Compassion and Self-Hate.</u> Touchstone, 1998.

Sanford, John, A. <u>Ministry Burnout.</u> New York: Paulist Press, 1982.

Schrage, Wolfgang. <u>The Ethics of the New Testament.</u> Philadelphia: Fortress, 1998.

Seamands, David, A. <u>Healing for Damaged Emotions.</u> Chariot Victor Publishing, 1991.

Sermon Title: "God's Antidote To Busyness," 2004.

Shay, Jonathan. <u>Odysseus in America: Combat Trauma and the Trials of Homecoming.</u> Scribner, 2002.

Sittler, Joseph. <u>The Maceration of the Minister. In Grace Notes and Other Fragments,</u> selected and edited by Robert M. Herhold and Linda Marie Dellhoff. Philadelphia: Fortess, 1981.

Silverman, David. <u>Doing Qualitative Research: A Practical Handbook</u>. Thousand Oaks, CA: Sage Publications, 2000.

Spaite, Daniel and Debbie Salter Goodwin. <u>Time Bomb in the Church: Defusing Pastoral Burnout.</u> Missouri: Beacon Hill Press of Kansas City, 1999.

Stone, Howard and James Duke. <u>How to Think Theologically</u>. Minneapolis: Fortress, 1996.

Swindoll, Charles R. <u>Stress: Calm Answers for the Worry Worn.</u> Portland: Lockman Foundation, 1977.

Trull, Joe E. and James E. Carter. <u>Ministerial Ethics. Being a Good Minister in a Not-so-Good World.</u> Nashville: Broadman, 1993.

Unger, Merrill F. <u>The New Unger's Bible Dictionary.</u> Chicago: Moody Press, 1988.

U.S. Army Chief of Chaplains. <u>The U.S. Army Chaplaincy Strategic Plan FY 2000-2005.</u> Washington, D.C.: Government Printing Office, August, 2000.

Vickery, Donald, D. and Fries, James, F. <u>Take Care of Yourself,</u> 4th ed. Addison-Wesley Publishing Company, Inc. Massachusetts, 1989.

Walvoord, John F. and Zuck, Roy B. <u>The Bible Knowledge Commentary: New Testament.</u> Colorado Springs, Victor, 2000.

Weber, Stu. <u>Four Pillars Of A Man's Heart.</u> Oregon: Questar Publishers, Inc., 1997.

Whitney, Donald S. <u>Spiritual Disciplines for the Christian Life.</u> Colorado Springs: NavPress, 1991.

Williamson, Lamar, Jr. <u>Interpretation of Mark: A Bible Commentary for Teaching and Preaching.</u> John Knox Press, Louisville, 1983.

Zoroya, Gregg, USA Today: <u>A fifth of soldiers at PTSD risk.</u>, 7 March 2008.

Printed in the United States
by Baker & Taylor Publisher Services